RICK WARREN
GENERAL EDITOR

better
together
What on earth are *we* here for?

PurposeDriven®
20 Empire
Lake Forest, California 92630

PurposeDriven®

Published by Purpose Driven® Publishing.
20 Empire
Lake Forest, CA 92630
www.purposedriven.com

The phrase Purpose Driven® is a registered trademark of Purpose Driven® Ministries.
All rights reserved.

TABLE OF CONTENTS

We're Called To Serve Together

We're Created to Worship Together

40 Days of Community Study Guide

Small Group Resources

Dear Friends,

During *40 Days of Purpose* we discovered that God placed each of us on earth for five purposes: to get to know and love him (worship), to learn to love each other (fellowship), to grow in becoming like Jesus (discipleship), to practice using our talents in serving God (ministry), and to share the Good News with others (evangelism). Today, millions of people around the world have begun to enjoy living a purpose driven life.

But this life of purpose that God intends for you is not meant to be lived alone. In fact, it is impossible to fulfill God's five purposes for your life by yourself. We need each other! From the beginning, God's plan has been that you will fulfill his purposes in community with other people—people in your church family, in your small group, and in the world around you. Why did God plan it this way? Because we're better together!

The goal of *40 Days of Community* is to water the seeds of purpose that were planted in your life during *40 Days of Purpose,* and help you take the next step to spiritual maturity and a meaningful life on earth. *40 Days of Community* will deepen your understanding of how God uses other people—specifically others in your church family—for your good and your growth. It will also show you how God can use you to bless others.

Our focus for the next 40 days will be on fulfilling God's five purposes together. We'll do this two ways: first, by deepening the community of love within our church family, and second, by reaching out in love to the community around our church family. Both are essential for a healthy, balanced, purpose-driven life.

Your participation in this small group will be the most essential part of *40 Days of Community*. Real community (koinonia) is caught, not taught. In your group, you'll not just learn how to build community—hopefully, you'll experience it.

40 Days of Purpose focused on the question: "What on earth am I here for?" Now we're ready to look at a second question: "What on earth are *we* here for?" During the next six weeks, we'll examine the five reasons we need each other to fulfill God's purposes for our lives. Here's an overview of the reasons:

We fellowship better together! The Bible says you were formed for fellowship, and obviously you can't fellowship by yourself! It takes at least two people. At the same time, you can't fellowship with a crowd either. True fellowship happens in a small group of people. That's why Jesus had a small group of twelve disciples! He modeled fellowship.

Community doesn't happen automatically. And joining a church doesn't guarantee fellowship! You can attend church services your entire life and still feel lonely and disconnected. The Bible says, "You must learn to be considerate of one another, cultivating a life in common" *(1 Corinthians 1:10, Msg)*. Notice that fellowship is something we must learn how to do. It must be intentionally cultivated.

What does it mean to cultivate a life in common? In the Bible, the Greek word for fellowship is "koinonia." It means to be as committed to each other as we are to Jesus Christ. Real fellowship takes us beyond simply socializing or studying together and into deeper levels of serving together and, at times, even suffering together. That kind of fellowship is the antidote to the pervasive loneliness that haunts so many people.

We grow better together! Just as your hand can't grow if it gets severed from your body, you cannot grow spiritually if you are detached from fellowship with a local body of believers. The Bible says that together we are the Body of Christ. And as such, every member of the body is important and necessary for the body to function as it was designed to do.

During *40 Days of Community* we'll practice some of the best ways to help each other grow spiritually, such as accepting each other *(Romans 15:7)*, affirming each other *(1 Thessalonians 5:11)*, and advising each other *(Colossians 3:16)*. Just as a baby needs a family in order to grow, you need a spiritual family in order to become all God intends for you to become.

Some people think that the only way to be holy or righteous is to live in isolation—become a hermit in a cave so you won't be stained by humanity. But Jesus, the most holy person who ever lived, lived among us—in the middle of all our problems. He comforted the poor, hung out with outcasts, touched lepers, and associated with people with all kinds of hang-ups and bad habits. Religious leaders called him "the friend of sinners," a derogatory term, but Jesus considered it evidence of his love.

It's only in community that we learn life's most important lesson—learning how to love. Without relationships, we'll never be able to develop patience, kindness, unselfishness, forgiveness, and all the other Christlike qualities that God wants us to possess.

We serve better together! Paul urged the believers in the church at Philippi, *"Then make me truly happy by agreeing wholeheartedly with each other, loving one another, and working together with one heart and purpose" (Philippians 2:2, NLT).* There are many benefits to serving God together instead of by yourself: we compensate for each other's weaknesses, we're more efficient, we multiply our effectiveness, we can defeat bigger problems, and we can support each other when we're tired or discouraged.

Did you know that your talents are not for your benefit? God gave them to you for the benefit of others. And he gave others talents for your benefit. That way, none of us can arrogantly claim that we are completely self-sufficient. God wants us to depend on each other to accomplish his purposes.

In fact, our talents are best used when we combine them with the talents of others. As the Bible says, *"Two people can accomplish more than twice as much as one; they get a better return for their labor" (Ecclesiastes 4:9, NLT).* Serving God together is the way he intended, and during *40 Days of Community*, many of us will experience the joy of serving together for the very first time.

We worship better together! Worshiping together increases our joy, enlarges our perspective, helps others to believe, and guarantees God's presence in our midst. Jesus said, *"Whenever two or three of you come together in my name, I am there* with you" *(Matthew 18:20, CEV)*. While it is true that God is always with us, there is a unique and powerful sense of his presence that can only be enjoyed and experienced in community with other believers.

When we worship with other believers it helps us see beyond ourselves and our own problems. C.S. Lewis, the brilliant Oxford author, was asked about the importance of worshiping together. He told about his first experience in attending worship services: "I very much disliked their hymns, which I considered to be fifth-rate poems set to sixth-rate music. But as I went on, I saw the great merit of it all . . . and gradually my conceit began peeling off. I realized that the sixth-rate hymns were, nevertheless, being sung with devotion and benefit by an old saint in elastic-side boots in the opposite pew, and I realized that I wasn't fit to clean those boots. Worshiping together gets us out of our solitary conceit."

We reach out better together! The Bible says, *"Above all else, live in a way that brings honor to the good news about Christ . . . Then I will know that you are working together and struggling side by side to get others to believe the good news" (Philippians 1:27, CEV)*. God expects us to partner in sharing the Good News with others.

One practical way you can do this is by inviting people from your community to be a part of this small group study with you! Many people who might be reluctant or hesitant to visit a church service would gladly accept an invitation to an informal group study in a home or office. Don't miss this perfect opportunity to reach out to neighbors, friends and co-workers.

Another way your small group can reach out together is through a group outreach project. There are plenty of opportunities right in your own community: the poor who need to be fed, shut-ins who need a visit, the elderly who could use some help around the house with repairs or yard work, kids with a single parent who need mentors, and people all around you who need to know that God loves them and has a purpose for their lives. That's why he sent Jesus to die for them.

Jesus tells us in *Matthew 25:35-40 (NIV)* that one day we'll each stand before God and one of the things we'll be evaluated on is how we treated other people: *"I was hungry and you gave me something to eat, I was thirsty and you gave me something to drink, I was a stranger and you invited me in, I needed clothes and you clothed me, I was sick and you looked after me, I was in prison and you came to visit me."* We'll say, "When did we do that to you, Lord?" And God will reply, *"Whatever you did for one of the least of these . . . you did for me."*

It's time for us to put our love into action. Imagine what could happen if every small group in your church reached out together, showing love in practical ways to those in your community. Don't you think that would make a difference in your area?

Now imagine what could happen if every small group in all the purpose driven churches across the country did it with you! Millions of lives would be touched, millions of people would begin a relationship with Christ, millions of practical needs would be met, and the church would become known more for the love it shows than for what it is against. God would be pleased, and we could see a spiritual awakening that is desperately needed in our culture.

God is moving in amazing ways in thousands of churches these days. I invite you to be a part of making history! It is an invitation to become a part of a great movement of purpose driven people and churches who are living for the global glory of God. Someone once pointed out that snowflakes are frail, but when enough of them stick together they can stop traffic. In the same way, you and I may feel like we can't make much of a difference as individuals. But together— with others in your small group, and with your church family, and with other congregations that are also committed to God's purposes—we can make a difference in our culture and our world. That is the awesome power of community!

It is no accident that you are a part of this *40 Days of Community*. Before you were born, God chose you to be a difference-maker and to make an impact for good with your life. Are you willing to take the next step in growing a life of purpose and meaning? Then let's join together for this 40 day spiritual journey— deepening the community of love within your church and reaching out in love to the community around your church.

We are better together!

With love and admiration for you,

Rick Warren

Rick Warren

A word about this workbook:

This *40 Days of Community* workbook contains everything you'll need for your journey. It includes…

- Your 40 daily devotional readings, based on 40 "one anothers" from the Bible. These short daily readings will support what your pastor teaches each weekend and what you study in your small group each week.

- Your journaling pages where you can write down the things you learn and the actions you take as a result of the daily readings, your group study, and the messages by your pastor. You can share these insights with your small group.

- Your study guide and materials for your weekly small group gatherings. Be sure to bring this workbook with you for each small group meeting.

During these next 40 days, I urge you to cut back on television intake and any other activities that could distract you from getting the most out of this journey together.

BETTER TOGETHER
Devotions and Journal

BECAUSE GOD LOVES US

"Since God so loved us, we also ought to love one another."
1 John 4:11 (NIV)

Life is about learning to love.

The purpose of your time on earth is not primarily about acquiring possessions, attaining status, achieving success, or even experiencing happiness. Those are secondary issues. Life is all about love and developing relationships—with God, and with other people. You may succeed in many areas, but if you fail to learn how to love God and love others, you'll have missed the reason God created you and placed you on this planet. Learning to love is life's most important lesson. Jesus called it the *"greatest commandment"* (Matthew 22:38, NIV). Nothing else comes close in importance.

Why? Because God is love, and God wants you to become more like him. God loves you deeply and unconditionally. Now he wants you to learn to love him back, and to love others, especially believers in God's family.

Here's the problem: Love is unnatural for us. It is human nature to think of ourselves first. We naturally do what is in our own best interest, often without any regard for how it affects others. Hopefully, as we grow we become more giving and less selfish; but we've all known people who never grew up and never considered anything but their own wishes, desires, and cravings. Self-centeredness is the root of practically every problem—both personally and globally.

Real love is placing the needs of others before your own. It is making your problem, my problem. It is giving to another without any guarantee of getting anything back. It is giving others what they need, not what they deserve. Although love can create intense feelings, love is not a feeling. It is a choice, an action, a way of behaving, a commitment. Love is sacrificing for others.

Much of the world has no clue as to what real love is all about. Songs that say "I need you, I want you, I must have you" are not love songs, but lust songs. Real love focuses on how I can serve you, not how you can serve me. It's the opposite of our selfish tendencies.

That's why we must *learn* to love. It isn't easy. Real love takes knowledge, God's grace, and lots of practice. We must retrain ourselves to think and act in loving ways. During *40 Days of Community* we're going to practice loving each other—in 40 different ways. These ways are called the "one anothers" of the Bible. They are practical instructions for learning to love in real-life situations.

Like a diamond, love is multi-faceted. Each of these daily readings will help you understand and practice a different aspect of love. Take the time each day to seriously think about what you've read. Learning genuine love is not easy, but it will bless your life beyond imagination here on earth, and prepare you for eternity.

Of course, you can't learn to love by yourself. You must develop relationships with many different kinds of people in order to practice loving others. The Bible calls this being in "community", which is another word for fellowship. To practice the "one another" commands that God has given us, it is absolutely essential that you find a church family and get involved in some kind of weekly small group study. An effective small group is more than just a Bible study, although that is a major component. It also allows time for interacting, sharing, questioning, and praying for each other. Community is the context where we learn to love.

If all you do is read these daily devotionals, you'll only get a fraction of the potential benefits. But if you meet weekly in a small group setting, with six or eight other people, you'll have a practice lab where you can apply what you learn.

Now here's today's verse: *"Since God so loved us, we also ought to love one another" (1 John 4:11, NIV).* This is the starting point for building real community: realize how much God loves us. He doesn't just love you; he loves everyone else just as much, and he wants his children to love each other. There are three foundations for living a life of love:

- God's love *for* us gives us the reason to love others.

- God's love *in* us gives us the ability to love others.

- God's love *through* us gives us the way to love others.

POINT TO PONDER:
Life is about learning to love.

VERSE TO REMEMBER:
"We love because God first loved us."
1 John 4:19 (TEV)

QUESTION TO CONSIDER:
How comfortable are you with being in a *40 Days of Community* small group?

Day 1 Journal

Day 2

BECAUSE GOD COMMANDS IT

"A new command I give you: Love one another. As I have loved you,
so you must love one another."
John 13:34 (NIV)

Love is an act of our will.

God says we must *decide* to love one another. We're to love other believers regardless of how we feel about them or how unlovable they may appear. No matter how difficult it may seem, we're to actively, consistently, and deeply love the believers God brings into our lives, our congregations—and our small groups.

Love is a command. Our decision to love is an act of obedience. God considers loving one another so important that he told us we *must* do it *(1 John 4:21)*. It is a lesson so important that the Apostle John consistently describes love and obedience as synonymous: if you love Jesus, you will obey his commands *(John 14:15, 23-24; 15:12, 14, 17; 1 John 2:3; 5:3; 2 John 1:6)*.

Why is obeying connected with love? Because it reflects unity among believers— a oneness of spirit within our congregations and small groups that is foundational to kingdom work: *"The message you heard from the very beginning is this: we must love one another"* (1 John 3:11, TEV). Christ crushes the myth that love is based upon thinking nice thoughts or feeling gushy emotions. He pushes the definition of love to a higher level—where behavior and beliefs combine into godly action. Love is no longer a schoolyard romance or a relationship dictated by compatibility; rather, real love is, and has always been, a mother stumbling to her baby's crib for the fifth time in one night, or a passenger giving up his place on a lifeboat to save someone else from a sinking ship. Love is Christ on a cross, dying for us—

even while we were still lost in our sins *(Romans 5:8)*.

Jesus requires us to view other people as highly valued children of God, well worth our time, attention, and energy. As members of God's family, we must choose to love, not who to love.

Love requires community. We cannot obey Christ's command in isolation. We have to be connected to each other in order to "love one another." Being in community forces us to drop our "relationship fantasies"—where everyone we know is easy to get along with and every conflict is resolved in happy compromise.

God shaped each one of us differently, and he knows we all bring different perspectives and needs into any community. The hurts, habits, and hang-ups present in any group create potential for conflict, but God's design is to use that conflict to help us grow in Christ.

Love carries high standards. Jesus says we are to be to one another what he is to us. The love of Christ is selfless, sacrificial, and submitted to the Father's will. His standard of love is personal—reaching out to the undeserving, looking past their faults and into the desperate needs of their hearts.

His standard is so staggering we can only reach it by faithfully adapting Galatians 2:20: It is no longer just I who *loves*, but Christ who *loves* in me. And this unlovable person that I now love, I love by the faith of the Son of God, who loved this unlovable one first and gave himself up for this person I am seeing as undeserving of love.

The bottom line is this: as a purpose driven community of believers, our love is not to be measured by the minimum of what we can do, nor is it to be limited to only those who appear deserving. Our standard for real love is that God "... *loved us and sent his Son as a sacrifice to take away our sins ... Since God loved us that much, we surely ought to love each other*" (1 John 4:10-11, NLT).

POINT TO PONDER:
Love is an act of the will.

VERSE TO REMEMBER:
"A new command I give you: Love one another. As I have loved you,
so you must love one another."
John 13:34 (NIV)

QUESTION TO CONSIDER:
**How can you show the selfless love of Christ to
an unlovable person in your life today?**

Day 2 Journal

_____

_____

_____

_____

_____

_____

_____

_____

_____

_____

_____

_____

_____

_____

_____

_____

_____

_____

BECAUSE IT IS HOW WE LOVE GOD

"People who don't love other believers, whom they have seen, can't love God, whom they have not seen."

1 John 4:20b (GW)

We love God by loving others.

The believers around us are important to God, so they should be equally important to us. In fact, saying we love God, but not loving other believers, is a lot like saying, "I like you, but I don't like your wife."

The Bible says, *"Everyone who loves has been born of God and knows God. Whoever does not love does not know God, because God is love"* (1 John 4:7b-8, NIV). If we can't love the people sitting right next to us in church, how can we claim to love God, who is in heaven?

The essence of love is not what we think or do or provide for others, but how much we give of ourselves: *"Be full of love for others, following the example of Christ who loved you and gave himself to God as a sacrifice to take away your sins" (Ephesians 5:2, LB)*. Our love compels us to set aside our own needs in order to give ourselves extravagantly toward meeting the needs of the other believers in our small groups and congregations. Loving one another means we yield our preferences, comfort, goals, security, money, energy, or time for the benefit of someone else.

We love God when we see each other the way God sees us. This means we stop judging others according to appearances and start viewing them from a heavenly perspective *(2 Corinthians 5:16)*. This Christ-sight allows us to see the things God sees, such as in John 4, where Jesus meets the woman at the well.

Judging by appearances, she was a woman with a long history of sin, rejected by her own people because of her past and by the Jews because of her ethnicity. But Jesus saw her true value and her desperate need, and he filled her with his living water.

We love God when we become doers of the Word, and not mere hearers: *"Anyone who listens to the word but does not do what it says is like a man who looks at his face in a mirror and, after looking at himself, goes away and immediately forgets what he looks like" (James 1:23-24, NIV)*. The fact is, it is possible to diligently study the Scriptures, yet have no understanding of God's love *(John 5:39-40)*.

It's nearly impossible to sit in a church pew absorbing Scripture for 30 years but doing little for those around you, and still claim to love God. The Bible says, *"The man who says, 'I know him,' but does not do what he commands is a liar, and the truth is not in him. But if anyone obeys his word, God's love is truly made complete in him. This is how we know we are in him: Whoever claims to live in him must walk as Jesus did" (1 John 2:4-6, NIV)*.

The Bible says we should show love whenever we have the opportunity *(Galatians 6:10)*, using every chance we get *(Ephesians 5:2)*. Were you aware that God is constantly placing people right in front of you so you can have these opportunities to demonstrate love? Today could mark a new beginning in your life as you open your eyes and begin looking for the opportunities God sends your way.

The Bible teaches, *"Never tell your neighbors to wait until tomorrow if you can help them now" (Proverbs 3:28, TEV)*. Why is now the best time to express love? Because you don't know how long you'll have the opportunity to express it. Circumstances change. People die. Children grow up. You have no guarantee of tomorrow. If you want to express love, you need to do it now.

Knowing you will one day stand before God, here are some questions you need to consider:

* • How will you explain those times when projects or things were more important to you than people?

• Who do you need to start spending more time with?

• What do you need to cut out of your schedule to make that possible?

• What sacrifices do you need to make?

POINT TO PONDER:
We love God by loving others.

VERSE TO REMEMBER:
"People who don't love other believers, whom they have seen, can't love God, whom they have not seen."
1 John 4:20b (GW)

QUESTION TO CONSIDER:
What does the way you show love to others say about your love for God?

Day 3 Journal

BECAUSE IT SHOWS WE'RE SAVED

"We know that we have passed from death to life, because we love other believers."
1 John 3:14 (GW)

Loving other believers is the evidence that we belong to God's family.

Our love for other believers is the fruit flowing from our relationship with God, but it is important to understand it does not establish our relationship with him: *"For it is by grace you have been saved, through faith—and this not from yourselves, it is the gift of God—not by works, so that no one can boast"* *(Ephesians 2:8-9, NIV).*

When we become members of God's family *(Ephesians 2:19)*, a death-to-life transformation moves us from being selective about who we love to being free and unconditional with our love. Anyone who loves in this way is *"born of God and knows God" (1 John 4:7, NLT)*, but without this Christlike love, we can't possibly claim to be part of God's family *(1 John 3:10).*

Consider this: if you have no love for others, and if you're only concerned about your own needs, then you should question whether Christ is really in your life. A heart transformed by God is a heart that loves. If you have doubts about your salvation, then one of the first questions to ask yourself is: Do I love other believers? If there is no fruit, you should question the root!

Can you point to a specific time in your life when you said "yes" to God and allowed Jesus to transform your heart? If your answer is no, then it's time to settle the issue today. Who are you going to live for—yourself or God?

You may hesitate, wondering whether you will have strength to live for God and to love like he's asking you to love, but don't worry—God will give you what you need once you make the choice to live for him and become a member of his family. The Bible says, *"Everything that goes into a life of pleasing God has been miraculously given to us by getting to know, personally and intimately, the One who invited us to God" (2 Peter 1:3, Msg).*

The first step in learning to love like Jesus starts by committing yourself completely to Jesus Christ. The Bible promises, *"To all who received him, to those who believed in his name, he gave the right to become children of God" (John 1:12, NIV).*

Will you accept God's offer?

First, believe. Believe God loves you and made you for his purposes. Believe you're not an accident. Believe you were made to last forever. Believe God has chosen you to have a relationship with Jesus. Believe in your heart that Jesus died on the cross for you and that God raised him from the dead *(Romans 10:9).* Believe that no matter what you've done in the past, God wants to forgive you.

Second, receive. Receive Jesus into your life as your Lord and Savior. Receive his forgiveness for your sins. The Bible says, *". . . whoever accepts and trusts the Son gets in on everything, life complete and forever!" (John 3:36a, Msg).* Wherever you are reading this, I invite you to bow your head and quietly whisper this prayer: "Jesus, I believe in you and I receive you." His Spirit will come into your life and will give you the power to love others with a godly standard.

If you sincerely meant that prayer, congratulations! Welcome to the family of God! You are now ready to discover and start living God's purpose for your life.

I urge you to tell the people in your small group about this decision so they can celebrate with you, pray for you, and help you grow in Christian maturity.

There may be others of you reading this who've already made a commitment to Jesus, but you realize now that you haven't been doing a very good job of loving other believers. That's OK—God will help you grow in your capacity to love. In fact, that will be one of the benefits of this 40 day study on community. You can use this devotional to agree with God that the *only thing that counts is faith expressing itself through love" (Galatians 5:6, NIV).*

POINT TO PONDER:
Loving other believers is evidence that we belong to God's family.

VERSE TO REMEMBER:
"We know that we have passed from death to life, because we love other believers."
1 John 3:14 (GW)

QUESTION TO CONSIDER:
If you were put on trial for your faith, and your expressions of love were the only evidence, what would the verdict be?

Day 4 Journal

BECAUSE WE'RE A FAMILY

"Love your brothers and sisters in God's family."
1 Peter 2:17b (NCV)

We long to belong.

Yesterday we learned that all believers *"belong in God's household with every other Christian" (Ephesians 2:19, LB)*. This means church is not something we go to, rather it's something we belong to—a family of God's people. It's more than an organization, more than an institution, even more than a group of like-minded people.

We are a family forged by the fires of God's love, and we are to *"be devoted to each other like a loving family" (Romans 12:10a, GW)*. We are to love one another like brothers and sisters. This sense of family togetherness allows us to create authentic Christian community—where we are accepted, supported, and challenged to fully live out the purposes of our lives. We belong, and we help others believe that they belong.

Family is synonymous with a deep, unwavering commitment to support one another no matter how rough it may get. You do things for family that you wouldn't do for anyone else, and you make allowances for family members that you might not make for anyone else.

For many of us, this image of family fails because we've never really been in a loving, wholesome family. We've only seen broken models, shattered relationships, and hurting hearts. The good news is that God wants to provide you with the very things you've longed for in a family, and he can do that in Christian community.

As we learn to love one another, our small groups can create the sense of family necessary to trust one another, accept one another, and serve one another. We learn the power of unconditional love. Our small groups are meant to be Holy Spirit-led laboratories for learning to love one another deeply and earnestly *(1 Thessalonians 4:9; 1 Peter 1:22)*.

How does our spiritual family teach us to love?

First, we learn to develop healthy relationships. We may have learned unhealthy methods of relating in our physical families, but in a community of believers we can see models of good relationships. We'll learn that it takes honesty, vulnerability, effort, and a lot of forgiveness to make relationships work.

Second, we learn to develop godly character. Character tends to be more caught than taught, and in Christian community we are able to see up-close and personal the character traits of others. We'll see maturity modeled, and we'll see immaturity displayed, and we may get to model or display some of that ourselves as we all learn and grow together.

Third, we learn the importance of biblical values. We've all picked up values intentionally and unintentionally. Some of these values may be right; some of them may be wrong. By bringing them into the family-setting of a Christian small group, we are able to measure our values against the standards of the Bible and in the context of mature Christian beliefs. *"One generation makes known your faithfulness to the next"* (Isaiah 38:19, LB).

You may be fortunate enough to have already seen healthy family relationships modeled in your home or in your congregation. But there are many of you who have emerged from shaky home environments. The next few weeks offer you an opportunity to break from the past. This is your chance to belong to a loving family, and to start fresh in developing healthy relationships, godly character, and biblical values.

This is your chance to choose your spiritual legacy, which will also transform your physical legacy. Don't leave it up to chance. Join your brothers and sisters, and learn to love deeply.

POINT TO PONDER:
Love must be learned.

VERSE TO REMEMBER:
"Love your Christian brothers and sisters."
1 Peter 2:17b (NLT)

QUESTION TO CONSIDER:
How devoted are you to your church family?

Day 5 Journal

BECAUSE IT IS PRACTICE FOR ETERNITY

"We are anxious that you keep right on loving others as long as life lasts,
so that you will get your full reward."
Hebrews 6:11 (LB)

The greatest lesson in life is love.

God designed life for us to learn how to love one another like God loves us. For the moment, we are in the midst of some rather serious on-the-job-training. God is making use of all things—pain and suffering, joy and comfort, opposition and cooperation—to transform us into people who love fully and deeply.

We're to spend our lives learning to love one another because God wants us to be like he is, and God is love: *"Whoever does not love does not know God, because God is love" (1 John 4:8, NIV).* God designed this life to sever our ties to self-centeredness so that he can teach us to be other-centered—putting the needs of others over our own.

This love we are learning will never die: *"Inspired speech will be over some day; praying in tongues will end; understanding will reach its limit"* *(1 Corinthians 13:8, Msg),* but the love we learn now will last forever. This life is practice for an eternity of love. It's like spring training in the game of baseball: we're practicing our love for one another now, strengthening our skills, preparing for the World Series of Love in heaven.

This is why we're spending 40 days focused on loving one another in community; the stakes are enormous and the results will last forever. This is God's purpose: *"... when the time is ripe he will gather us all together from wherever we are—in heaven or on earth—to be with him in Christ forever" (Ephesians 1:10, LB).* No doubt, we will be surprised in heaven by how our love has flowed into eternity *(Ephesians 4:4).*

In the meantime, we're to:

Love urgently. *"And we are anxious that you keep right on loving others as long as life lasts" (Hebrews 6:11, LB).* There is an urgency about learning to love now because today could be our last day on earth. This life is fleeting, and eternity is coming. The opportunities for us to express love come and go quickly; we cannot take them for granted. One day our earth-bound lessons will end, and we'll love for eternity in heaven.

Love consistently. As long as we're living, we're to *"keep right on loving."* This curriculum of love is not something we learn once, and then put behind us. We have to study it for a lifetime, until we *"know it so well, we've embraced it heart and soul."* We're to *"take up permanent residence"* in this life of love, where we *"live in God and God lives in us" (1 John 4:16, Msg).*

Love expectantly. We're to keep loving so we will get our *"full reward"* *(Hebrews 6:11, LB).* The greatest rewards in heaven will be for love, and those who love the most will be the most rewarded. It is in those we love where we will find our greatest reward.

POINT TO PONDER:
The greatest lesson in life is love.

VERSE TO REMEMBER:
"We are anxious that you keep right on loving others as long as life lasts, so that you will get your full reward."
Hebrews 6:11 (LB)

QUESTION TO CONSIDER:
How can you practice love more urgently, consistently, and expectantly?

Day 6 Journal

_____

_____

_____

_____

_____

_____

_____

_____

_____

_____

_____

_____

_____

_____

_____

Day 7

BECAUSE IT IS A WITNESS TO THE WORLD

"Your love for one another will prove to the world that you are my disciples."
John 13:35 (NLT)

The whole world is watching how we love one another.

Jesus gave the world the right to judge the authenticity of our faith by how much we love one another. We prove our faith in Christ, not by the rules we keep, but by the love we give. Notice Jesus didn't say, "Love me," as proof of our discipleship. He said, "Love one another, and that will show the world you belong to me." Our love for one another is a tangible and contagious reflection of God's love—allowing the world to witness the power of transformed lives.

The best thing we can do to reach our community for Christ is to love each other. As we love people into God's kingdom, we start first by loving other believers. Until the world sees the love of God modeled in Christian community, they're going to have trouble believing it could ever exist. When we truly care for one another, we show the world a love so tangible and contagious that they can't help but be attracted to it.

As the world watches, they'll see us *"...being of the same mind, maintaining the same love, ...intent on one purpose" (Philippians 2:2, NAS),* not merely looking out for our own personal interests, but also for each other's interests *(Philippians 2:3-4).* The world is desperate for love and a sense of community, and we're meant to be the salt *(Matthew 5:13)* that increases their thirst for the living water *(John 4:10).* *"Whoever believes in me, as the Scripture has said, streams of living water will flow from within him" (John 7:38, NIV).*

Our love for one another shows the world our unity with the Father, and also shows them that community requires unity—a oneness about the purposes of life. Jesus said to his Father, *"I want all [my disciples] to be one with each other, just as I am one with you and you are one with me. I also want them to be one with us. Then the people of this world will believe that you sent me" (John 17:21, CEV).*

This means the influence of our congregations is not about attendance, or buildings, or programs. Our influence within the greater community is based upon our love for one another. We make a statement about God by the way we love one another. It may be a positive statement or it may be a negative one, but the fact is people often form their opinions of God based upon our individual reputations: "You may be the only picture of Jesus people will ever see." Or, they may form their opinion of God based upon the reputation of our congregations—how we get along, how we support each other, how we criticize, how we love one another.

Isn't it alarming, then, to think that we're often known for what we are against, rather than by what we are for—the Good News of a love so *"wide and long and high and deep"* that it encompasses more than any of us could ever imagine *(Ephesians 3:18, NIV).* Our community of unity should reflect the faith we have in the love of Jesus Christ. Our small groups are meant to be points of love and light in the darkness of our communities. We're to let our *"light shine so that others will see the good"* and praise our Father in heaven *(Matthew 5:16, CEV).*

The world wants to know that the Good News of Jesus is true. This week's memory verse, *John 13:35,* tells us that our love for each other is the proof the world is looking for. People are less impressed with our words than they are with our actions of love for one another. Your love for one another speaks volumes about God's love: how loud is your voice?

VERSE TO REMEMBER:
"Your love for one another will prove to the world that you are my disciples."
John 13:35 (NLT)

QUESTIONS TO CONSIDER:
How loudly do your actions speak about the love of God?
How loud is the voice of your small group?

Con't. So, if I can't love him as a child of God, what does that say about me? Do I have real love for anyone?

How do we as a church deal with the sinful behavior of Don and Ryan. Do we have the right to "judge" the behavior as non biblical and confront based on that?

I know why Don reacts to me so negatively but why everyone else on the O.B.? Does he see everyone as his "mother who abandoned him"?

And if other people see how we let him go on behaving badly — how do we look to them? He causes the pain (sin) and we take the blame. How many do we sacrifice on this altar?

Day 7 Journal

I have struggled this week with the problem of loving Dan. His behavior Monday night at Official Board was ~~depol~~ deplorable. Yet we all just sit in stunned silence. Amber revealed some info about his dislike for the "Kory dynasty", which didn't cause me to be angry. I already sensed this, she just confirmed it. I completely understand that Dan must be in great pain to behave as he does, yet I'm not able to feel compassion for him. Why do we have to love him if he isn't working with the H.S. to allow transformation. Aren't we enabling him? When I behave badly, I recognize it, ~~and~~ pray for change. He justifies his action as our fault, never his. Is he a Christ follower? in the truest sense?

BY BEING INTENTIONAL

*"Be wise in the way you act with people who are not believers,
making the most of every opportunity. When you talk, you should always be kind
and pleasant so you will be able to answer everyone in the way you should."*
Colossians 4:5 (NCV)

Love cares about the destiny of others.

If you knew the cure for cancer or AIDS, and you kept it a secret, telling no one while millions continued to die, would that be loving? Of course not. If you knew the key to extending human life by 50 years, would you want to share it with others? Of course you would. But as believers who've learned the way to eternal life, we have an even more important, longer lasting, and urgent message to share with the world, and love leaves no choice.

How can we reach out to those in our community who don't know Christ? What's the best way as a small group and as a church family to share the Good News with our friends, relatives, neighbors, and co-workers? The starting point is to become *intentional* about it. We must choose to start caring about the eternal destiny of the people around us. Until we decide to care about those who aren't yet in God's family, we won't invest the time, prayer, and effort it takes to reach them for Jesus. It's easier to remain silent while people around us live and die without knowing Christ, but it is also unloving.

The Apostle Paul was a veteran at reaching out to nonbelievers because he cared about what God cares most about: people! In *2 Timothy 2:10 (NLT)*, Paul stated the depth of his love for those not yet a part of God's family: *"I am willing to endure anything if it will bring salvation and eternal glory in Christ Jesus to those God has chosen . . ."*

In *Colossians 4:5-6*, Paul shares the four ways we can become intentional about introducing others to Jesus:

First, he says, *"Be wise in the way you act"* with people who are not believers. That means being aware that everything you say and do is a witness for or against Christ. If you claim to be a follower of Christ, you will be watched closely by those who don't know him. They want to see how a believer acts—how you handle problems, irritations, delays, disappointments, and especially how you handle relationships. Does your faith cause you to smile at people? Are you optimistic and encouraging? When people let you down, are you gentle or judgmental? When you're frustrated, are you rude and arrogant with others or polite and patient? All of these responses to life are a witness.

Second, Paul says, *"make the most of every opportunity."* To make the most of them, you must first become aware of them. Ask God to open your eyes to see the daily occasions he gives you to share a simple word of testimony about the difference Jesus Christ has made in your life. Begin each day by praying "Jesus, help me to see and love people the way you do." Then read the Gospels to learn how Jesus interacted with people.

Making the most of every opportunity requires living in constant connection with Christ. Talk with him often throughout your day, and it will increase your sensitivity to the spiritual needs of people around you. Remember, God has never made a person he didn't love. The Bible says, *"[God] wants all people to be saved and to learn the truth"* (1 Timothy 2:4, GW).

A third way we reach out intentionally is to make sure our words are *"always kind and pleasant."* When you know the truth, it is tempting to be preachy and pushy with the gospel. But people are never argued into the family of God. They are attracted to it by love. You are never persuasive when you are abrasive. Be warm-hearted and gracious instead.

Finally, Paul says to be ready and *"able to answer everyone in the way you should."* That requires preparation and intentionality. For the rest of this week, we'll look at how to do this, but it begins with your decision to become aware, to care, and to share with the people God has placed in your life. *Colossians 4:5* is this week's memory verse. If you commit it to memory, then God will be able to remind you to be intentional.

POINT TO PONDER:
Make the most of every opportunity to share.

VERSE TO REMEMBER:
"Be wise in the way you act with people who are not believers, making the most of every opportunity."
Colossians 4:5 (NCV)

QUESTION TO CONSIDER:
Will anybody be in heaven because of you?

Day 8 Journal

Day 9

BY USING OUR SMALL GROUP

*"...you are working together and struggling side-by-side
to get others to believe the Good News."*
Philippians 1:27b (CEV)

"We" is more powerful than "me."

There is power in partnership, and that's never truer than when we're working to tell the world about Jesus. Evangelism is always a team effort, even in those times when we think we're working alone. The reality is, when we lead someone to Christ, the Holy Spirit has already been at work in that life, and other believers have also been influential, directly and indirectly. Paul once wrote, *"I planted the seed, Apollos watered the plants, but God made you grow" (1 Corinthians 3:6, Msg).*

We're to *"work together as partners who belong to God" (1 Corinthians 3:9, NLT),* because *"two can accomplish more than twice as much as one" (Ecclesiastes 4:9, LB).* That's the value of small groups—they allow us to work side-by-side in an effort to lead our friends and family members to Christ. Like the four friends who brought their paralyzed friend to Jesus *(Mark 2:1-12),* we can draw strength and encouragement from one another as we bring our own friends into his presence.

In fact, if you've never experienced the privilege and joy of helping someone come to Christ, today can be a turning point in your life—by grasping the fact that you can help bring other people to Jesus as part of a group effort. You don't have to do it alone; God intends for us to work together, side-by-side.

The first step to take in your small group is to pray together. Before we start to witness, we need to pray. We cannot pray for people and not become concerned about them. Here are four ways your group can pray for your non-believing friends and family members:

First, pray for an opportunity to talk about Jesus *(Colossians 4:3)*. Ask God to give you an opportunity to tell others about Christ, and to invite them to church. You don't have to doubt it—God will answer that prayer!

Second, pray that God will prepare the hearts of those you try to reach. Do you know how God softens hearts? He sends the rain. Anytime you see someone going through a storm in life, you can know God is softening that person's heart.

Third, pray for God to soften your heart. Say, "I'll be honest, God. I don't care that much about other people. I care about myself. I care about my own plans and priorities and my family." Soon God will fill your heart with a "burden," which is just an old-fashioned word that means your heart is now tender towards other people.

Fourth, pray that the words of Jesus *"will simply take off and race through the country to a groundswell of response" (2 Thessalonians 3:1, Msg.)*, just as they did among the early Christians.

Now, be inventive in the way your group invites those you are praying for into the group setting: have a barbecue, a movie night, a game night, dessert night—the possibilities are limitless. The Bible says this: *"Make the most of your chances to tell others the Good News. Be wise in all your contacts with them" (Colossians 4:5, LB)*.

Finally, here is a prayer you and your small group can use: "Father, we want you to use our group to 'reach one more for Jesus.' Develop in us a deep concern for people who don't know Jesus, and prompt us to pray consistently for their salvation.

We know you paid a high price to bring us into your family, and we agree with you that no one is hopeless or beyond the reach of your love. Guide us as we reach out in your name, and give an inventive creativity to our methods for outreach. Father, in faith we ask that in this next year our small group will be able to reach twenty people for you. We lift this prayer in the name of Jesus. Amen."

POINT TO PONDER:
"We" is more powerful than "me."

VERSE TO REMEMBER:
"...you are working together and struggling side by side
to get others to believe the Good News."
Philippians 1:27b (CEV)

QUESTION TO CONSIDER:
Which of your friends and family members can your small group begin praying for?

Day 9 Journal

BY OFFERING HOSPITALITY

"Open your homes to each other without complaining."
1 Peter 4:9 (TEV)

Open hearts lead to open homes.

< maturity >

For the Christian, hospitality is not an option. It is an injunction *(Isaiah 58:6-9; Luke 14:12-14)*. We're commanded to practice hospitality—from the example of the patriarch Abraham, who saw three holy visitors coming to him across the burning sands *(Genesis 18)*, all the way to the wise counsel of the Apostle Paul *(Romans 12:13b)*.

For some, hospitality is as natural as breathing. For others, the practice must be acquired. For all, the gift must be nurtured *(1 Peter 4:9)*.

Christ's ministry to this impoverished, captive, blinded, and oppressed world must, in one way or another, also be ours *(Luke 4:18-19)*. Many of us have been given a remarkable tool through which to minister—the miracle of a Christian home. If Christians would open their homes and practice hospitality as defined in Scripture, we could significantly alter the fabric of society. We could play a major role in its spiritual, moral, and emotional redemption.

Think of the impact the church could make in society if only four or five families in each congregation would care for needy children, nurturing them in love and pointing them to Christ. If a large urban area has a hundred churches, four or five homes times a hundred would involve at least four or five hundred children.

Many who say they follow Christ have no comprehension of the basics of hospitality. We've allowed the world to force us into its mold. Entertaining says,

Worship in the building.
Service outside the building

"I want to impress you with my beautiful home, my clever decorating, my gourmet cooking." Hospitality, however, seeks to minister. It says, "This home is not mine. It is truly a gift from my Master. I am his servant and I use it as he desires." Hospitality does not try to impress, but to serve.

Entertaining always puts things before people. "As soon as I get the house finished, the living room decorated, my place settings complete, my housecleaning done—then I will start having people in." "The So-and-so's are coming. I must buy that new such-and-such before they come." Hospitality, however, puts people before things. "We have no furniture; we'll eat on the floor."

Entertaining declares, "This is mine—these rooms, these adornments. Look, please, and admire." Hospitality whispers, "What is mine is yours" *(Acts 2:44)*.

Hospitality puts away pride and doesn't care if other people see our humanness. Because we are maintaining no false pretensions, people relax and feel perhaps we can be friends.

Today's church needs to be bathed in unselfish, loving, accepting hospitality. Unless we develop a true spirit of acceptance in our church families, the hospitality we extend to our world will be hypocritical. When our immediate homes and the household of God are what our Lord intended them to be, we will naturally extend an openness to our neighbors around us.

It is appalling how few Christians have entered into the lives of their immediate neighborhoods. These are a nearby inheritance to which our Father desires us to minister. How few of us are trying to find ways to serve our neighbors, to extend mercy. Often our official Christianity—our meetings and commitments—make us less accessible to them rather than more available.

If Christians, corporately, would begin to practice hospitality, we could play significant roles in redeeming our society. There is no better place to be about the redemption of society than in the Christian servant's home; and the more we deal with the captive, the blind, the downtrodden, the more we realize that in this inhospitable world, a Christian home is a miracle to be shared.

In Webster's Dictionary, the definition for hospitable is wedged between the word "hospice," which is a shelter, and the word "hospital," which is a place of healing. Ultimately, this is what we offer when we open our home in the true spirit of hospitality: we offer shelter; we offer healing.

Here are some practical steps toward hospitality:
- Request the presence of God as you open your home.
- Determine how your habits keep you from being more hospitable.
- Evaluate your gifts and how they can be used for hospitality.
- Be a host home for a small group.
- Join someone in team-hosting a dinner for friends.
- Take in a troubled teen.

POINT TO PONDER:
Open hearts lead to open homes.

VERSE TO REMEMBER:
"Open your homes to each other without complaining."
1 Peter 4:9 (TEV)

QUESTION TO CONSIDER:
Have you had your neighbors into your home lately?

Adapted from "Open Heart, Open Home: The Hospitable Way to Make Others Feel Welcome & Wanted" by Karen Mains. Copyright ©1997 by Karen Mains. Used by permission of InterVarsity Press, P.O. Box 1400, Downers Grove, IL 60515. www.ivpress.com

3-7-06

I was thinking about the double meaning of "opening our homes". Jesus used a house to represent "ourself" - the many rooms to represent the many parts of ourself. When Rick talks about opening our homes to the captive, the blind, downtrodden, etc., how effective it is to minister without all the masks and facades we typically hide behind. When we are transparent we are effective. This so perfectly describes "spiritual formation" as God's plan for our wholeness. It seems clear the Holy Spirit is leading us to intentional discipleship as a focus for our growth.

BY SHOWING ACCEPTANCE

Day 11

"Reach out and welcome one another to God's glory. Jesus did it; now you do it!"
Romans 15:7 (Msg.)

We are to accept others the way Jesus accepts us.

Jesus loves us even at our worst, demonstrating *"his own love for us in this: While we were still sinners, Christ died for us" (Romans 5:8, NIV)*. He accepts us among his beloved children *(Ephesians 1:6)*, despite our messy lives, impure motives, and irritating attitudes. His acceptance of us doesn't condone any sin; rather, it recognizes that we are God's workmanship—each of us is a uniquely-shaped child of God created for a specific purpose *(Ephesians 2:10)*.

One of the ways we love one another is by accepting each other just as Christ accepts us. This brings glory to God. *"Jesus did it; now you do it, too" (Romans 15:7b, Msg)*.

But our acceptance of others should also include nonbelievers, knowing that, while *they're* still sinners, Christ died for *them*. *"It isn't our job to judge outsiders" (1 Corinthians 5:12, LB)*. This doesn't mean we condone sin; yet so much of our rejection of those outside the church is based upon fear and our prejudice that people need to be like us before they can be with us.

Jesus was not afraid to be friends with nonbelievers *(Luke 19:7)*. He looked past the sin in their lives to see who God created them to be. He understood that accepting people is not the same thing as accepting their sins. As the old saying goes, "Love the sinner, not the sin." One of the best examples of Jesus doing this

bondage

is in the story of Zacchaeus, where Jesus found the hated tax collector sitting in a tree *(Luke 19:1-10)*. In this encounter we learn the characteristics of Christ-like acceptance:

First, no matter where you are, Jesus meets you there. We must accept nonbelievers in spite of the circumstances of their lives—looking at them like Jesus does, with eyes of love. Jesus knows everything they've ever done, everything they've ever said, everything they've ever thought, and yet he still loves and accepts them. And so should we!

One of the deepest expressions of love is attention. We show God's love to nonbelievers when we spend time with them. Time is a precious gift to anyone because it is something that can never be replaced. There are people all around us who are dying to be noticed, dying for someone to give them the gift of time. They need to know they matter to God, and that he created them on purpose and for a purpose.

Second, no matter what others call you, Jesus knows your name. While everyone else was putting Zacchaeus down as a sinner, Jesus called him by name and reached out to him with friendship. And this gift of friendship changed Zacchaeus' heart. Jesus wants us to do the same. He wants us to reach out to the lost with his love and acceptance. He wants us to see others as he sees them, and to draw them into his kingdom purposes through genuine love and friendship.

Third, no matter what you've done, Jesus won't reject you. Good behavior has never been a prerequisite for friendship with Jesus. He loves and accepts people, regardless of what they've done. He is far more interested in changing us than he is in condemning us.

If Zacchaeus was anything like the rest of us, he probably thought he wasn't good enough to invite Jesus to his home, but the reality is—Jesus has seen it all. No matter what you've done, Jesus still says, *"Those the Father has given Me will come to Me, and I will never reject them" (John 6:37, NLT).* Jesus not only has a plan and purpose for your life, he also has a plan and a purpose for those who don't yet believe in him. That's why he wants us to reach out and welcome others to God's family. *Gideon – God knew the person he was going to become.*

POINT TO PONDER:
God wants you to accept others just like Jesus accepted you.

VERSE TO REMEMBER:
"Reach out and welcome one another to God's glory. Jesus did it; now you do it!"
Romans 15:7 (Msg.)

QUESTIONS TO CONSIDER:
Who is the last person in your life that you would expect to become a Christian? How could your acceptance of them build a bridge to Christ?

Day 11 Journal

BY BUILDING FRIENDSHIPS

"Be friendly with everyone. Don't be proud and feel that you are smarter than others. Make friends with ordinary people."
Romans 12:16 (CEV)

"Become friends with God; he's already a friend with you" (2 Corinthians 5:20b, Msg).

That's the message we're to tell the world, but we limit ourselves in how we can share this Good News if our only friends are other believers. Jesus, on the other hand, understood his mission was to seek the lost, and so he became friends with those who needed to become friends with God.

The Bible says that when the Pharisees saw Jesus keeping company with disreputable characters, *". . . they had a fit, and lit into Jesus' followers. 'What kind of example is this from your Teacher, acting cozy with crooks and riffraff?' Jesus, overhearing, shot back, 'Who needs a doctor: the healthy or the sick? Go figure out what this Scripture means: "I'm after mercy, not religion." I'm here to invite outsiders, not coddle insiders'" (Matthew 9:10-13, Msg).*

Jesus knew his purpose, and that allowed him to relax around unbelievers. He wasn't worried when others accused him of being a friend of sinners *(Luke 19:7)* because he was doing exactly what the Father sent him to do: persuade men and women to make peace with God *(2 Corinthians 5:20)*.

Likewise, Jesus wants us to be his representatives, speaking on his behalf to those still on the "outside." Yet many Christians are so isolated and disconnected from unbelievers that they rarely have any meaningful conversations with them. The longer we're believers, the more insulated we tend to become from unbelievers.

And often, the more insulated we become from them, the more uncomfortable we become with them. In the end, we no longer have any friendships with the very people Jesus wants us to reach.

Jesus understood that our witness to nonbelievers starts with friendship: we earn the right to share the gospel through relationship. The bottom line is this: People don't care how much you know until they know how much you care. Nonbelievers, like most of us, are looking for deep, true, supportive friendships.

The Apostle Paul said we should try to find "common ground" with nonbelievers, so that we can tell them about Christ: *"I do this to get the gospel to them and also for the blessing I myself receive when I see them come to Christ"* *(1 Corinthians 9:21-23, LB)*. Searching for common ground expresses an attitude of friendliness—where we look for the positive instead of the negative in those outside the faith.

When Jesus began talking to the woman at the well *(John 4:4-26)*, he searched for common ground rather than condemning her. As a result, she not only made peace with God, she also brought her friends and family into the presence of Jesus. We see from this example that our friendship with nonbelievers requires that we understand the difference between loving them and loving their ways.

In *John 3:16a (Msg.)*, we're told, *"This is how much God loved the world: He gave his Son, his one and only Son."* Clearly, God loves people—the people of the world—but that's not the same thing as loving the values of the world. We're told: *"Don't love the world's ways. Don't love the world's goods. Love of the world squeezes out love for the Father"* *(1 John 2:15, Msg)*.

Building friendships requires:

- Courtesy: *"Always talk pleasantly and with a flavor of wit, but be sensitive to the kind of answer each one requires"* (Colossians 4:6, NJB).

- Frequency: You've got to spend time with nonbelievers in order to become friends with them.

- Authenticity: *"Love from the center of who you are; don't fake it. Run for dear life from evil; hold on for dear life to good"* (Romans 12:9, Msg).

POINT TO PONDER:
Love the people of the world, but not the values of the world.

VERSE TO REMEMBER:
"Be friendly with everyone. Don't be proud and feel that you are smarter than others. Make friends with ordinary people."
Romans 12:16 (CEV)

QUESTION TO CONSIDER:
Do you have any meaningful friendships with nonbelievers?

Day 12 Journal

Day 13

BY GIVING PRACTICAL HELP

"Little children, let us stop just saying we love people;
let us really love them, and show it by our actions."
1 John 3:18 (LB)

People know we love them when we show we love them.

Jesus stopped. He stopped when people needed his help, when they needed his comfort, when they needed his protection, when they needed an answer to a perplexing problem. Jesus saw the interruptions in his life as divine opportunities to show God's love to people in desperate need.

Jesus approached love from a show, then tell perspective. He defined love as meeting needs, and when he touched people, they realized *"...they were in a place of holy mystery, that God was at work among them. They were quietly worshipful—and then noisily grateful, calling out among themselves, 'God is back, looking to the needs of his people!'" (Luke 7:16, Msg).*

Jesus expressed his love through action. He calls us to be action figures, but he never wants us so busy saving the world that we ignore the interruptions of those in need. Like the Good Samaritan, Jesus wants us ever ready to set aside our agenda in order to help someone in need *(Luke 10:25-37)*. The Bible says, *"If you see some brother or sister in need and have the means to do something about it but turn a cold shoulder and do nothing, what happens to God's love? It disappears. And you made it disappear" (1 John 3:17, Msg).*

Jesus showed that faith and service go hand-in-hand. When the woman of poor reputation anointed Jesus' feet with expensive oil and tearfully washed them with her hair, Jesus said to her, *"Your faith has saved you. Go in peace"* (Luke 7:50, NIV). Her act of service was a reflection of her faith in God.

When the disciples of John the Baptist asked Jesus to verify he was the Christ, his response was to point to his service. He said, *"Go back and report to John what you have seen and heard: The blind receive sight, the lame walk, those who have leprosy are cured, the deaf hear, the dead are raised, and the good news is preached to the poor"* (Luke 7:22, NIV).

As James later taught, we are to be doers of the word, not just hearers: *"Does merely talking about faith indicate that a person really has it? For instance, you come upon an old friend dressed in rags and half-starved and say, 'Good morning, friend! Be clothed in Christ! Be filled with the Holy Spirit!' and walk off without providing so much as a coat or a cup of soup—where does that get you? Isn't it obvious that God-talk without God-acts is outrageous nonsense?"* (James 2:14b-17, Msg).

Otherwise, we amputate the Body of Christ, cutting off the arms and legs so that all is left is one big mouth: *"What a strange thing a body would be if it had only one part!"* (1 Corinthians 12:19, NLT). Francis of Assisi once wrote, "Preach the gospel, if necessary, use words."

In showing our love, no task should be too menial. Jesus specialized in acts of service most people try to avoid: washing feet, helping children, fixing breakfast, and serving lepers. Nothing was beneath him, because his service flowed from his love.

Jesus indicated our acts of love should be very practical; even giving a cup of cold water in his name is an act of love *(Matthew 10:42)*. There are so many needs in the world; simply look around and begin to address what you see:

- Help mow someone's lawn
- Watch a neighbor's child
- Bring food to a shut-in
- Care for the sick
- Begin to ask, "How can I serve you today?"

We serve God by serving others, and we can serve even better together (*Ecclesiastes 4:9*). Consider how your small group can work together to help those around you.

POINT TO PONDER:
People know we love them when we show we love them.

VERSE TO REMEMBER:
*"Little children, let us stop just saying we love people;
let us really love them, and show it by our actions."*
1 John 3:18 (LB)

QUESTION TO CONSIDER:
Who can you share the love of Christ with in a practical way today?

Day 13 Journal

Day 14

BY REPRESENTING JESUS

"Whatever you do or say, let it be as a representative of the Lord Jesus."
Colossians 3:17 (NLT)

". . . I no longer live, rather Christ lives in me" (Galatians 2:20, NIV).

As believers, our role in life has changed. We no longer have the assignment of looking out for our own interests. Our job now is to represent the interests of Jesus. We are to be his face and hands and feet—showing up in the lives of others on his behalf. We represent Jesus in the hospital; we represent Jesus at the funeral; we represent Jesus at the wedding; we represent Jesus across the fence as we talk to our neighbors.

We are not of this world, but we are in this world. We function as ambassadors for Christ *(2 Corinthians 5:14-21)*; we serve at the will of King Jesus. We serve as spokesmen and servants for God's Kingdom—always prepared to give an explanation about the hope we have *(1 Peter 3:15)* while still remembering this world is not our home *(1 Peter 2:11)*.

We reach nonbelievers by living in such a way that they ask us about the King we represent. As ambassadors of Christ, we work hard to understand the culture in order to translate our King's message in such a way that those alien to his kingdom will understand his commandments and his policy of grace.

Our ambassadorship is more than a mere job; it is our highest calling. But in order to be faithful ambassadors, we have to make a very simple, yet critical decision: do we want to impress nonbelievers, or do we want to influence them?

If our objective is to impress them, then we can do that at a distance, but that also leaves the Kingdom of God at a distance. If we want to influence nonbelievers, we have to get close enough for them to see our faults and frailties, but that's also where they will see our faith as real and necessary.

Do you think God wants you to impress nonbelievers or influence them?

Here are some ways to extend your influence as a representative of Jesus:

- By smiling at people. The Bible says a cheerful look brings joy to the heart *(Proverbs 15:30)*. You can influence others with a simple smile.

- By sympathizing with people. We can offer emotional support and encouragement for people in distress. *"[God] comforts us every time we have trouble, so when others have trouble, we can comfort them with the same comfort God gives us" (2 Corinthians 1:4, NCV)*.

- By serving people. The more you serve others in love, the more you will influence them. The Apostle Paul wrote, *"Even though I am free of the demands and expectations of everyone, I have voluntarily become a servant to any and all in order to reach a wide range of people" (1 Corinthians 9:19, Msg)*.

- By speaking up. Being a representative of Christ requires courage; we're to let people know we believe. His love not only compels us to explain our faith, it will sometimes prompt us to confront evil behavior in others. *"Let the redeemed of the Lord say so" (Psalm 107:2, NASB)*.

• By sacrificing. *". . . Christ was sinless, and he offered himself as an eternal and spiritual sacrifice to God . . . Now we can serve the living God and no longer do things that lead to death"* (Hebrews 9:14, CEV). Great sacrifice equals great influence, and that may mean your influence will increase only after you move out of your comfort zone. If your sacrifice helps change the world, is it worth it?

Pray today: "God, I want to be your representative. I want you to use me to influence every person I come in contact with today, showing them the depth and breadth of your love."

POINT TO PONDER:
We no longer live, rather Christ lives in us.

VERSE TO REMEMBER:
"Whatever you do or say, let it be as a representative of the Lord Jesus."
Colossians 3:17 (NLT)

QUESTION TO CONSIDER:
How can you represent Jesus in your world today?

Day 14 Journal

_____

_____

_____

_____

_____

_____

_____

_____

_____

_____

_____

_____

_____

_____

_____

_____

_____

BY ADMITTING OUR NEED FOR EACH OTHER

"Since we are all one body in Christ, we belong to each other,
and each of us needs all the others."
Romans 12:5b (NLT)

We need each other.

Recently, there was a news report about Jim Sulkers, a Winnipeg, Manitoba, resident, who died in his bed and laid there for two years before his neighbors in the same complex discovered it. The man had lived there 20 years, but no one missed him.

Why are we so reluctant to admit our need for each other? There are two powerful reasons:

First, our culture glorifies individualism. We admire independent, self-sufficient people who seem to get along quite well by themselves. But the sad truth is, beneath that confident appearance is usually a lonely and insecure person with a heart filled with hurt. Loneliness is the most common disease in the world, yet we continue to build walls instead of bridges between each other.

Second, we have pride. Many people, especially men, feel it is an admission of weakness to ask for help or to express a need. But there is absolutely no shame in needing others. God wired us that way! He wants his children to depend on each other.

In *The Purpose Driven® Life*, we learned that God intends for us to experience life together. (If you haven't read that book yet, it's important that you do.) We were designed for relationships. We were formed for fellowship in God's family and created for community. It is not God's will that you go through life by yourself. Even in the perfect, sinless environment of Eden, God said, *"It is not good for the man to be alone" (Genesis 2:18, NIV).*

God hates loneliness. That does not mean everyone should be married. It does mean everyone needs a spiritual family, and that's why God created the church. When God saves you and adopts you into his family, he intertwines your life with the lives of other believers. You're not just a believer, you are a belonger. *"Now all of you together are Christ's body, and each one of you is a separate and necessary part of it" (1 Corinthians 12:27, NLT).*

The word "body" is often used to describe a group of people connected for a purpose. In school, you were part of a student body. Elected political leaders form legislative bodies. But when God calls the church "the Body of Christ," he has a human body in mind where every part is interconnected and interdependent. *"The body we're talking about is Christ's body of chosen people. Each of us finds our meaning and function as a part of his body" (Romans 12:5a, Msg).*

And, like parts of any living body, it's impossible for believers to thrive without each other. *"Can you imagine Eye telling Hand, 'Get lost; I don't need you'? Or, Head telling Foot, 'You're fired; your job has been phased out'?" (1 Corinthians 12:21b, Msg).*

You must be connected to a church fellowship to survive spiritually. More than that, you need to be in a small group of people where you can love and be loved, serve and be served, share what you're learning and learn from others. You can't do that with a crowd.

Since we're called by God to fellowship together, this week we'll look at ways to build community with our brothers and sisters in God's family. The first step is to admit we need each other, living like our spiritual lives depend on each other—because they do!

"Be devoted to one another in brotherly love. Honor one another above yourselves" (Romans 12:10, NIV). Living in community requires humility. We must continually remind ourselves that we belong to each other and need each other. Memorizing *Romans 12:5*, this week's memory verse, will help remind you.

POINT TO PONDER:
I need other believers in my life and they need me.

VERSE TO REMEMBER:
"Since we are all one body in Christ, we belong to each other, and each of us needs all the others."
Romans 12:5b (NLT)

QUESTION TO CONSIDER:
What might be keeping you from making a deeper commitment to your small group?

Day 15 Journal

BY COMMITTING TO EACH OTHER

"Let us agree to use all our energy in getting along with each other."
Romans 14:19a (Msg.)

Community is built through commitment.

A healthy Christian community is committed to loving each other, working with each other, and staying with each other. The Bible says, *"You can develop a healthy, robust community that lives right with God and enjoy its results only if you do the hard work of getting along with each other, treating each other with dignity and honor" (James 3:18, Msg).*

This is more than a superficial, "to each his own" approach to getting along. It means we see the value of each individual in our small group; we see each other as God's creations and as vessels of God's grace. It means we commit to being there for each other, *"none of this going off and doing your own thing"* (Colossians 3:15b, Msg).

God created us for this kind of commitment; he's committed to us, and he expects us to be committed to him and then to each other *(2 Corinthians 8:5)*. It's by God's design that we define our lives by our commitments: marriage, children, work, church.

Building a community of commitment takes time. It means living life together beyond our weekly meetings and making each other a priority—sharing our lives over coffee, after work, at the ballpark, in the hospital.

It means moving beyond superficial friendships and becoming *"a friend who sticks closer than a brother" (Proverbs 18:24, NIV)*. We're to focus on the quality of our relationships, not the quantity. We don't need a lot of friends in this life, but we do need a few good ones. In our small groups, we can be that to each other.

Committing to one another means:

- Loving no matter what. We're to love and support each other at all times, not just when it's convenient *(Proverbs 17:17)*; we're to love other people even at their worst, not just when we see them as loveable *(Romans 5:8)*.

- Being there for each other. A basic sign of commitment is simply showing up. If we care, we'll be there. Our presence is a source of encouragement *(Hebrews 10:25)*, but being there also means we're engaged in the lives of others. The martyred missionary Jim Elliot once said, "Wherever you are, be all there."

- Benefiting each other. God gives each of us unique abilities for the purpose of sharing them with others: *"Everyone gets in on it, everyone benefits" (1 Corinthians 12:7, Msg)*. Our small groups and our congregations are poorer if we do not freely use our spiritual gifts for the benefit of all. Commitment means we recognize each other as parts of a greater body working together *(Romans 12:4-5)*.

Who—or what—are you committed to? And who knows it? Have you ever gone to anyone, besides your spouse, and said, "I want you to know that I will always be there for you"? Have you ever established an intentional commitment to someone, saying, "I want to grow close to you as a friend"? Would you do that in your small group this week?

POINT TO PONDER:
Community is built through commitment.

VERSE TO REMEMBER:
"Let's agree to use all our energy in getting along with each other."
Romans 14:19a (Msg.)

QUESTION TO CONSIDER:
If you were to ask one of your good friends what—or who—they think
you are committed to, how do you think they would answer?

Day 16 Journal

Day 17

BY RESPECTING EACH OTHER

"Excel in showing respect for each other."
Romans 12:10b (GW)

Respect begins with a godly perspective.

Respect means we see one another through our Father's eyes as eternal beings *(John 3:16)* chosen by God *"for the high calling of priestly work . . . God's instruments to do his work and speak out for him . . ." (1 Peter 2:9, Msg)*. It also means seeing each other as *"heirs of God and co-heirs with Christ" (Romans 8:17, NIV)*.

Respect means we consistently remember we'll soon be sharing heaven with those in our small groups and congregations, even those we have difficulty respecting now. God *"put the body together in such a way that extra honor and care are given to those parts that have less dignity" (1 Corinthians 12:24, NLT)*.

A significant part of showing respect is simply listening. We offer our presence and open our ears—listening to the hidden hurts and heartaches, the deepest dreams and desires of one another. The God of the universe listens to our prayers; Jesus listened to those around him; we should listen to our brothers and sisters in Christ.

Part of listening means we don't rush to fix things or to give an answer; we respect others enough to let them share their full story. Sometimes all we need is for someone to hear what's on our hearts. Respect means we trust others, instead of assuming they will do it wrong, or not do it as well as we would *(Philippians 2:3)*.

We also demonstrate respect by the way we talk about others when they're not around. Nothing destroys relationships faster than gossip *(Proverb 16:28)*.

Respect means, instead of listening to or spreading rumors, we do everything we can to protect the reputation and dignity of our brothers and sisters in Christ. The Bible teaches that *"love covers over a multitude of sins" (1 Peter 4:8, NIV).*

We excel in showing respect when we work hard at being:

- Tactful, not just truthful. Tactfulness is thinking before you speak, knowing that the way you say something will influence how it is received. Criticism is best received when it is presented in a loving manner, and as mature Christians, we're to *"know the whole truth"* but *"tell it in love" (Ephesians 4:15, Msg).* Before you speak frankly with someone, ask yourself, "Why am I saying this? Will my words build them up or tear them down?" *"Kind words bring life but cruel words crush your spirit" (Proverbs 15:4, TEV).*

- Understanding, not demanding. We respect others when we treat them the way we would want to be treated *(Luke 6:31).* When people are dealing with you, do you want them to demand or understand? We should be considerate of one another's feelings and stresses: sometimes people don't feel good, and they're having a bad day. The Bible says, *"A wise, mature person is known for his understanding" (Proverbs 16:21, TEV).* The best place to practice this is in our homes and small groups. Often we're more polite to strangers than we are to the people we see every day.

- Gentle, not judgmental. Even when we disagree with one another, we should still be courteous and respectful—focusing on our own behavior first: *"... each of us will give an account of himself to God. Therefore let us stop passing judgment on each other. Instead, make up your mind not to put any stumbling block in your brother's way" (Romans 14:12-13, NIV).*

• Polite, not rude. When others are rude to you, you don't have to respond with rudeness. As Christ-followers, we are taught to respond with kindness: *"Don't let evil get the best of you; get the best of evil by doing good" (Romans 12:21, Msg).*

One final note on respect: God entrusted the pastors and spiritual leaders of your church to *"watch over your souls,"* and they are accountable to God for this task *(Hebrews 13:17, LB).* They must correctly teach God's Word; confront false teaching before it spreads; proclaim the Gospel to nonbelievers; pray for all people, including you and your family; train and appoint leaders; and they must do this all while serving as an example of what it means to be a follower of Jesus *(1 and 2 Timothy; Titus).*

Being tactful, understanding, gentle, and polite doesn't come easy for most of us. But it is all very necessary. In your journaling today, think about these things, and ask God for the strength of the Holy Spirit to enable you to *"excel in showing respect for each other" (Romans 12:10b, GW).*

POINT TO PONDER:
Respect begins with a godly perspective.

VERSE TO REMEMBER:
"Excel in showing respect for each other."
Romans 12:10b (GW)

QUESTION TO CONSIDER:
Which of the four ways of showing respect to others presents the greatest challenge to you?

Day 17 Journal

BY SUPPORTING EACH OTHER

"... all of you should be of one mind, full of sympathy toward each other, loving one another with tender hearts and humble minds."
(1 Peter 3:8, NLT)

God enables us to love the fear out of one another.

We drive fear from our community by loving one another so supportively that each member feels safe inside the group *(1 John 4:18)*. This safety allows us to bring our humanity into the group—including all our joy and pain, our ups and downs, our victories and defeats.

We give to one another the same uncommon safety Christ gives us—to be real, to be sad, to be messed up and confused, yet, to be loved. God challenges us to create a community where we love like our lives depend upon it *(1 Peter 1:22, Msg)*. and where we can each "live and move and have our being" *(Acts 17:28, NIV)*.

God wants us to weep as one and celebrate as one—caring for each other equally *(1 Corinthians 12:25-26)* as we comfort and confront, warm and warn, cherish and challenge within an atmosphere of supportive safety. He wants us to support each other with tender hearts and humble minds.

Tender hearts: We give support because God gave us support, and we're to encourage others with the encouragement we received from him *(2 Corinthians 1:4)*. We exhibit tender hearts when we say to one another:

It's OK to have a bad day;

It's OK to be tired;

It's OK to admit your mistakes;

It's OK to say your marriage is failing;

It's OK to confess your addiction;

It's OK to share you're scared;

It's OK to want a day away from your toddler;

It's OK to grieve this loss;

It's OK to doubt, to be confused, to cry.

Humble minds: Humble people aren't focused on how little they think they're worth, and they don't concern themselves with acting humble. Behavior like that is actually self-centered and reflective of false humility. Our humility should be a natural outgrowth of our loving spirit, where we see, through God's eyes, the value of others. True humility also means we understand our own value in Christ, and our own unique purpose. This allows us to celebrate the successes of others, knowing God blesses each of us in different ways and at different times, according to our needs and according to our mission. We exhibit humble minds when we say to one another:

It's OK be happy you got a new car;

It's OK to celebrate that you got a HUGE raise;

It's OK to joyfully tell us you lost 17 pounds;

It's OK to say you won the sales competition;

It's OK to shout "Hallelujah" because God's presence in your life is so good.

We demonstrate a tender heart when we weep with those who weep. We demonstrate a humble mind when we rejoice in the blessings of others as though they were our own.

Supporting each other also means we see each other for what we can be, not for what we appear to be now. Jesus called Peter a "rock" when the fisherman was still acting on impulse *(Matthew 16:18)*, and God called Gideon a mighty man of courage when he was hiding from the enemy *(Judges 6:11-12)*. We encourage and build each other up *(1 Thessalonians 5:11)* when we see others in terms of their purpose and mission in life.

As we seek *"ways in which we can support one another" (Romans 14:19, NJB)*, it might be helpful to remember that the word "support" literally means to "lend strength to." We find strength in places that are supportive, places where it's safe to be ourselves. What would that look like in your small group?

POINT TO PONDER:
God enables us to love the fear out of one another.

VERSE TO REMEMBER:
"... all of you should be of one mind, full of sympathy toward each other, loving one another with tender hearts and humble minds."
1 Peter 3:8 (NLT)

QUESTION TO CONSIDER:
To whom will you lend your strength today, and how will you do it?

Day 18 Journal

BY GETTING ALONG WITH EACH OTHER

"I beg you in the name of the Lord Jesus Christ to stop arguing among yourselves.
Let there be real harmony so that there won't be splits in the church.
I plead with you to be of one mind, united in thought and purpose."
1 Corinthians 1:10 (LB)

Stop trying to win arguments.

Instead, make it your goal to love those who disagree with you. Go for the love, not the win. Jesus tells us love will always win; he guaranteed that when he walked out of the tomb.

When you find yourself in an argument with other believers, use these biblical guidelines for getting along:

Let mercy guide your response *(Proverbs 3:3-6)*. In a conflict, most of us say we only want what's fair, but God's approach isn't about being fair. It's about grace and mercy *(Romans 5:8)*.

Let God determine the truth *(2 Corinthians 13:8)*. The truth is not determined by your thoughts or feelings *(1 John 4:1)*, or the opinions of others. Truth is what God says it is; he is the lone authority for interpreting any situation *(2 Corinthians 10:5)*.

Look for God's presence *(Matthew 28:20)*. Satan wants us to believe we're in the battle alone. Simon Peter provides an example of fighting alone: his use of blustery words, swords, curses and lies were all desperate attempts to care for himself; he fought as a man separated from God *(Matthew 26:52)*. But we should follow the example of the young shepherd boy, David, who believed God was in the fight and that the battle belonged to the Lord *(1 Samuel 17:47)*.

Lean on the mind of Christ *(1 Corinthians 2:15-16)*. The Bible says we shouldn't rely on our own understanding *(Proverbs 3:5)*, that what appears to be right to us may very well be wrong *(Proverbs 14:12)*.

Look for the conflict's true source *(Ephesians 6:12)*. According to God's Word, we're really not fighting other people; our real enemy is Satan and his *"unseen spiritual forces of wickedness."*

Lay down human weapons *(2 Corinthians 10:4-5)*. When we try to meet our own needs, working independently of God, we tend to use what the Apostle Paul called weapons of the flesh. These include: manipulation, gossip, slander, ridicule, threats, blame, nagging, deception, and silence. When we use them, we end up in an "evil for evil" cycle, and that's like trying to fight a skunk with "stink"—everybody loses!

Learn to use spiritual weapons *(2 Corinthians 10:4)*. The Bible tells us that prayer is a powerful spiritual weapon. After we put on the whole armor of God, we're to *"pray in the Spirit on all occasions with all kinds of prayers and requests"* *(Ephesians 6:18, NIV)*. Many Christians never think to pray together when an argument breaks out; yet prayer reminds us who God is and who we are as his children. Prayer puts an eternal perspective on any argument.

Forgiveness is another spiritual weapon. The power of forgiveness is greater than anything the enemy can use against you. It is God's command that we forgive others as we have been forgiven *(Matthew 6:12)*.

We don't always have to agree to get along. Our verse today says, *"Let there be real harmony.*" In an orchestra, there's a big difference between unison and harmony. If all the musicians played in unison all the time, the music would get pretty boring. It's the harmony that creates beauty in music, with different players playing different instruments and different notes, but all under the direction of one conductor. The goal of each musician is not to play louder than the others or to finish the piece first; the goal is to *"be of one mind, united in thought and purpose."* When this happens, the music is heavenly.

POINT TO PONDER:
Go for the love, not the win.

VERSE TO REMEMBER:
"I beg you in the name of the Lord Jesus Christ to stop arguing among yourselves. Let there be real harmony so that there won't be splits in the church. I plead with you to be of one mind, united in thought and purpose."
1 Corinthians 1:10 (LB)

QUESTION TO CONSIDER:
If you have a conflict with a brother or sister in Christ, what will you do today to seek reconciliation?

Day 19 Journal

BY BEING PATIENT WITH EACH OTHER

*"Be patient with each other, making allowance
for each other's faults because of your love."*
Ephesians 4:2b (NLT)

The more we understand, the more patient we become.

When we see the hurt beneath the anger, or the reason behind the behavior, we're more likely to *"make allowance for each other's faults."* The ability to understand is a sign of patience *(Proverbs 14:29)*. The Bible teaches, *"A man's wisdom gives him patience; it is to his glory to overlook an offense" (Proverbs 19:11, NIV)*.

It helps when facing a patience-challenge to remember God will never ask you to give more patience to others than the patience he gives to you. The Apostle Paul uses his own life as an example of this, saying God showed him mercy, despite his many sins, so that *"Christ Jesus might display his unlimited patience" (1 Timothy 1:16, NIV)*. When we connect our own patience to the patience of Christ, we're able to cut each other some slack; we agree with the wisdom that love is patient *(1 Corinthians 13:4)*, and that impatience is not love.

We need patience with one another because God created each of us with different shapes, assigning each of us a different mission in life. We all have different backgrounds, and we're each at a different place in our journey with Jesus. Practicing patience lifts your perspective, helping you to see our diversity as a strength, and not a weakness.

The Apostle Paul wrote, *"Welcome with open arms fellow believers who don't see things the way you do. And don't jump all over them every time they do or say something you don't agree with—even when it seems that they are strong on opinions but weak in the faith department. Remember, they have their own history to deal with. Treat them gently"* (Romans 14:1, Msg).

Work at being patient all the time. Anybody can be patient when it's convenient—but it's much harder to remain patient when the day is slipping away, or when it's the same mistake for the third time in one week. Being patient demands a cost; we have to set aside our agenda and yield our rights in order to *"welcome each other with open arms."*

One of the most practical steps toward real patience is learning to listen. This means more than just hearing someone else; it means to carefully and fully listen. The Bible says, *"Listen before you answer. If you don't you are being stupid and insulting"* (Proverbs 18:13, TEV). That's pretty clear! It means we shouldn't evaluate what someone has done, or what we hear, until we've heard the full story. God gave us two ears and one mouth, perhaps to tell us we should listen twice as much as we talk.

Ask yourself these questions:
- What are the things that make me impatient?
- What does my impatience over those things say about my priorities?
- How can I better understand the people who bring out my impatience?
- Have I taken time to listen to their full story?
- In what ways do people have to be patient with me?
- Do I give the same amount of grace to others as I expect others to give me?

First Corinthians 13:4 (NIV) says, *"Love is patient."* That means it puts up with a lot for a long time. The next time your patience reaches its limit, remember how patient and understanding Christ has been with you.

POINT TO PONDER:
The more we understand, the more patient we become.

VERSE TO REMEMBER:
"Be patient with each other, making allowance for each
other's faults because of your love."
Ephesians 4:2b (NLT)

QUESTION TO CONSIDER:
How can you become more patient with the people in your life?

Day 20 Journal

BY BEING HONEST WITH EACH OTHER

"No more lies, no more pretense. Tell your brother the truth. In Christ's body we're all connected to each other. When you lie to others, you end up lying to yourself."
Ephesians 4:25 (Msg.)

Honesty strengthens community.

Honesty deepens our relationships, allowing us to be transparent with one another *(Proverbs 24:26)*. It keeps our community open and authentic, freeing us to speak the truth in love *(Ephesians 4:15)* as we practice remarkable integrity *(Titus 2:7)*. It keeps us sensitive to the Holy Spirit's guidance *(John 16:13)* and helps us battle deceptions that could corrupt our lives in Christ *(2 Corinthians 10:5)*.

Honesty requires us to say what we mean and mean what we say *(Matthew 5:37)*. We're to show the same honesty in public as we do in private *(Acts 20:20)*. We're committed to one truth, not many *(John 14:6)*.

There are to be *"no more lies."* As new creations in Christ, we've taken off our old selves, and accordingly, we should no longer lie to each other *(Colossians 3:9)*. The devil is the father of lies: *"There is no truth in him. When he lies, it is consistent with his character; for he is a liar . . ."* *(John 8:44, NIV)*. People who push away the truth are sinful and wicked *(Romans 1:18)*, but we know the truth, and the truth has set us free *(John 8:32)*.

There are two kinds of lies:

- Lies of commission—These are lies where we specifically make false statements, but the Bible says we're to *"put off falsehood and speak truthfully"*

(Ephesians 4:25, NIV). We don't want to become liars who have *"lied so well and for so long"* that we've *"lost . . . capacity for truth"* *(1 Timothy 4:2, Msg.)* and see it only as *"a distant memory"* *(1 Timothy 6:5, Msg).*

- Lies of omission—These are lies where we fail to tell the whole truth, or we wink at the deceptions of others. These lies are characteristic of the *"smooth-talk"* used in Paul's time to gain entry into *"the homes of unstable and needy women" (2 Timothy 3:6, Msg.)* for the purpose of taking advantage of them. *"In the end, people appreciate frankness more than flattery" (Proverbs 28:23, NLT)*. We honor one another when we give an honest reply *(Proverbs 24:26, NLT).*

There is to be *"no more pretense."*

"We refuse to wear masks and play games. We don't maneuver and manipulate behind the scenes. And we don't twist God's Word to suit ourselves. Rather, we keep everything we do and say out in the open, the whole truth on display, so that those who want to can see and judge for themselves in the presence of God" (2 Corinthians 4:2, Msg). There should be no need to *"read between the lines or look for hidden meanings"* because we speak a *"plain, unembellished truth" (2 Corinthians 1:13, Msg).*

In fact, we're to *"use our powerful God-tools for smashing warped philosophies, tearing down barriers erected against the truth of God, fitting every loose thought and emotion and impulse into the structure of life shaped by Christ" (2 Corinthians 10:5, Msg)*.

Otherwise, dishonesty will pollute our lives together, and it will be difficult to develop a deeper trust for one another *(Luke 16:10, NLT)*. For instance, we may think going back on our word in some matters is minor, but it could end up causing problems throughout the entire congregation. The New Testament records such an incident at the church in Galatia, when the Apostle Peter told some new Christians one thing but then did something entirely different *(Galatians 2:12)*. His actions threatened the faith of a congregation filled with brand new believers, so Paul *"had a face-to-face confrontation with him because he was clearly out of line" (Galatians 2:11, Msg)*.

"Finally, brothers, whatever is true, whatever is noble, whatever is right, whatever is pure, whatever is lovely, whatever is admirable—if anything is excellent or praiseworthy—think about such things" (Philippians 4:8, NIV). For God says one day, *"Every tongue will tell the honest truth that I and only I am God" (Romans 14:11b, Msg)*.

POINT TO PONDER:
Honesty strengthens community.

VERSE TO REMEMBER:
"No more lies, no more pretense."
Ephesians 4:25a (Msg.)

QUESTION TO CONSIDER:
Which temptation are you more prone to struggle with: lies of commission or lies of omission?

Loaves & fishes

Individuation process

Generational Curses

Day 21 Journal

_____

_____

_____

_____

_____

_____

_____

_____

_____

_____

_____

_____

_____

_____

_____

_____

_____

BY BEING EXAMPLES TO EACH OTHER

"Join with others in following my example, brothers,
and take note of those who live according to the pattern we gave you."
Philippians 3:17 (NIV)

We all need models to mature.

Many people make the mistake of thinking all they need to grow spiritually is God's Word and prayer. But the truth is, we need people to help us grow. Christlike character is built through relationships, not in isolation. There are many things God wants you to learn about life that you'll never learn on your own. You'll only learn them in community.

We always grow faster and stronger with living, breathing examples who can model for us what a purpose driven life looks like. We need more than explanations, we need examples. Paul realized the power of a pattern when he advised, *"Join with others in following my example, brothers, and take note of those who live according to the pattern we gave you" (Philippians 3:17, NIV).* To grow, we need to see principles in practice. We need to see what beliefs look like when they are translated into behavior in everyday situations.

When Paul would travel to a city to start a church, he would begin by simply living among the people. He was a "living Bible," reflecting the life of Jesus in whom *"the Word became flesh and made his dwelling among us" (John 1:14, NIV).* Paul lived out the truth of the word in his own flesh as he dwelled among the people. After Paul left a city, he would write back, *"Keep putting into practice all you learned from me and heard from me and saw me doing, and the God of peace will be with you" (Philippians 4:9, NLT).*

Who are your models for following Christ? Who are you watching and learning from? Here's a tougher question: Are you an example for anyone else? In elementary school, you probably enjoyed "Show and Tell." As believers, we're often better at "telling" than "showing."

In today's culture, the world desperately needs people who can show us how to love our spouse and make a marriage last; how to relate to our kids; how to do business with integrity; how to handle conflict like Jesus would. These are lessons we learn by watching others.

Not only do we need models to grow, we also need mentors. Mentors are people who've followed Christ longer than we have and are able to share their life lessons. You've heard that it's wise to learn from experience, but it is wiser to learn from the experiences of others. Life is too short to learn everything by experience! And some painful experiences can be avoided if you're smart enough to learn from models and mentors in your church family.

Ask yourself this: "What's been the greatest positive influence on my life?" Most likely it was not a sermon, seminar, or Sunday school lesson. It was somebody who shaped your life through a personal relationship.

Can you see God's wisdom in creating the church, a family full of mentors and models for our benefit? This is why being connected to a small group is so crucial to spiritual growth. It's a regular opportunity to learn from each other.

Today, spend a few moments getting intentional about this. Write down the names of people in your church and small group that you'd like to learn from. Then identify what specifically you'd like to learn from them. They don't have to be perfect to be a model or mentor. If perfection were a requirement, no one but Jesus could help us.

To grow spiritually, you must also be willing to be a model or mentor to others. That may scare you, but all it takes is being one step ahead of the person you are mentoring. People don't expect you to be perfect—they already know you aren't. What they want you to be is honest! So let them see your struggles, not just your successes. We usually grow as much from other's weaknesses as we do their strengths.

POINT TO PONDER:
We all need models to mature

VERSE TO REMEMBER:
"Follow my example, as I follow the example of Christ."
I Corinthians 11:1 (NIV)

QUESTIONS TO CONSIDER:
Who will I look to as models and mentors for my spiritual growth?
Who am I willing to be an example to?

Day 22 Journal

BY ENCOURAGING EACH OTHER

"Encourage one another and build each other up."

1 Thessalonians 5:11 (NIV)

We have the power to kill or give life.

Many of the messages we hear from the world are the killing kind. We're told: "You're not smart enough; you're not thin enough; you're not fast enough; you're not GOOD enough." The Bible says, *"Words kill, words give life; they're either poison or fruit—you choose" (Proverbs 18:21, Msg).*

In a world where people are beat up and put down, we can provide a counter-balance to the negativity. We have the power to give life by telling one another: "You matter to me. Your life counts and has purpose. God loves you, and you're incredibly valuable to him." Our words may be the only encouraging thing some people hear in a day. We can become the voice of God's grace in their lives—helping with encouraging words *(Romans 14:19b).*

We see an example of this in Luke 13, where Jesus heals a woman who's been unable to stand up straight for 18 years. When the leaders in the synagogue question his healing on the Sabbath, Jesus says he's freeing a *"daughter of Abraham"* from the bonds of Satan. He doesn't describe her as an elderly, crippled woman, rather as an honored child of the Jewish nation. But more importantly, he places her desperate need—her spiritual and physical condition—in priority over the routines of the day.

Can you imagine what a blessing it was for her to hear those words? Jesus healed her physically, but he also built her up. She was a beloved daughter of

Abraham, worthy of notice, and significant enough to help immediately and not just at the designated times.

In the New Testament, the word "encouragement" often means "to come alongside." We're to come alongside one another, *"building each other up,"* just as the Holy Encourager comes alongside us to teach us and remind us of the way of Jesus *(John 14:26).*

We become encouragers when we stop looking down and in and start looking up and out. All we have to do is look around—the need and opportunity for encouragement is everywhere. *"Each one of us needs to look after the good of the people around us" (Romans 15:2a, Msg),* and this *"will build them up" (Romans 15:2b, NLT).*

So, how about it? This week, will you become a consistent source of encouragement to those around you? It's a choice on your part: you can lift a person's spirit, change the atmosphere of your office, or lighten the burden of someone in your small group. The Bible says we should *"look for the best in each other, and always do your best to bring it out" (1 Thessalonians 5:15b, Msg).*

The best place to begin is in our small groups, where we regularly come together to build each other up. Like building a muscle, we strengthen one another when we exercise our choice to encourage. Here are some steps to get you started:

- Commit to encouragement. From this day forward, agree: "I'm going to build up the people around me." Can you imagine the impact that would have? The name of Paul's companion, Barnabas, literally meant "son of encouragement." What kind of influence would you have if you committed to being a son or daughter of encouragement?

• Value other people. In the past several weeks of *40 Days of Community*, we've seen again and again that people are valuable to God; and if they are valuable to him, they should be valuable to us. An encourager works hard at bringing out the best in others.

• Focus on what's really important. When Jesus healed the *"daughter of Abraham,"* he focused on what was really important. In order to become an encourager, you may have to change your priorities, adjust your agenda, and focus on the fact that people are more valuable to God than our crammed-up schedules.

May your conversation this week be peppered with phrases like: "I believe in you …," "I'm grateful for you …," "I see God using you …," "I appreciate you …," and "I'm glad you are in my life." Be encouraged, there is good news of great joy for all people, and his name is Christ the Lord.

POINT TO PONDER:
We have the power to kill or give life.

VERSE TO REMEMBER:
"Encourage one another and build each other up."
1 Thessalonians 5:11 (NIV)

QUESTION TO CONSIDER:
How can you become a more consistent source of encouragement to those around you?

Day 23 Journal

BY TEACHING EACH OTHER

Day 24

"Let the words of Christ, in all their richness, live in your hearts and make you wise. Use his words to teach and counsel each other."
Colossians 3:16a (NLT)

We are all teachers of the faith.

We may be good teachers or we may be bad teachers, but we are teachers. Everyday, hopefully, we model biblical behaviors and respond with Christlike attitudes. The Bible sees us as teachers and encourages us to teach one another. In writing to an ordinary group of believers, the Apostle Paul states, *"I know that you have all the knowledge you need and that you are able to teach each other"* *(Romans 15:14b, NCV).*

Some of us are carrying around this myth in our minds that the only people who can teach are the gifted and the professional, but nothing could be further from the truth. We each have something to offer our friends and our small group. As we share our insights on a Bible passage, as we offer counsel from our experiences, as we call the group to pray in a time of crisis, we are teaching.

Teaching involves more than unpacking Bible stories or giving theological insight; we also teach when we help one another know how to love a spouse, make wise decisions, keep our thought-life pure, or get out of debt.

Paul says we're to *"counsel each other."* That means we should be learners, also—listening to other believers as they tell us about God's work in their lives, and watching one another to see what *"Christ in you"* looks like in another human being *(Colossians 1:27, NIV).*

King Solomon, a man the Bible says was the wisest person to ever live, said it is vital to learn from our friends *(Proverbs 12:15)*. Solomon wrote in *Proverbs 15:22 (NLT)*, *"Plans go wrong for lack of advice; many counselors bring success."*

In today's verse, Paul gives us an outline for how we can teach and learn from each other:

- Let the words of Christ live in your heart. We must know God's Word before we can teach it. As we hear, read, study, memorize, and meditate on the words of Christ, we take them into our hearts. This makes us wise and gives us the knowledge we need in order to teach one another *(Romans 15:14b, NCV)*.

- Use God's words to teach and counsel each other. It's more than just human insight or experience that we're to pass on to others. Whenever Paul wrote to a congregation, he challenged the believers to teach and encourage each other with God's truth. Too often we look to the world's conventional wisdom when we're seeking answers; yet it is the world who desperately needs the spiritual wisdom found in God's Word.

Of course, once we learn from the wisdom of God, we must correctly apply it in our lives, holding tight, not relaxing our grip: *"Guard it well—your life is at stake!" (Proverbs 4:13, Msg)*.

Your small group provides an excellent opportunity for every member to develop skills as a leader and teacher. Consider rotating who facilitates the discussion each week, or rotating who leads certain sections of the small group meeting. This will help and encourage each member to grow in their faith and gifts. The

Bible says, *"Take your turn, no one person taking over. Then each speaker gets a chance to say something special from God, and you all learn from each other"* (1 Corinthians 14:30-31, Msg).

Your small group relationships are not coincidental. It is not by accident that God placed you in a particular small group for this 40 Day study on community. There are things that your group will learn only from you, and things you will learn that could've only come from people in your small group. What an incredible privilege! The God of the universe has chosen you to speak into the lives of your friends, and provided you with friends who are able to speak into your life.

POINT TO PONDER:
We are all teachers of the faith.

VERSE TO REMEMBER:
"Use his words to teach and counsel each other."
Colossians 3:16a (NLT)

QUESTION TO CONSIDER:
What are some lessons God has taught you recently that you can share with your small group?

Day 24 Journal

BY WARNING EACH OTHER

"Exhort one another every day, as long as it is called 'today,' that none of you may be hardened by the deceitfulness of sin."
Hebrews 3:13 (ESV)

If you care, you share.

"It's none of my business" is not a Christian phrase. It is your business. Just as *"iron sharpens iron" (Proverbs 27:17, NIV)*, we're to push each other toward Christlike behavior and protect one another from failing in our faith. We need people in our lives who will love us enough to warn us when necessary.

As we studied last week, God wants us to *"tell each other the truth, because we all belong to each other in the same body" (Ephesians 4:25, NCV)*. Note the basis for telling the truth and for warning each other is that *"we all belong to each other."*

Our warnings are not to be mere rebukes; they should be positive and redemptive—calling us to a higher place and reminding us of our godly purpose. They are exhortations for restoration, and are given as loving corrections with a humble heart and compassionate words. The Apostle Paul said, *"So be on your guard! Remember that for three years I never stopped warning each of you night and day with tears" (Acts 20:31, NIV)*. Can you hear the passion and compassion in his voice? When our warnings are motivated by love and based on committed relationships, they rarely come across as harsh or mean. In fact, they tell others how much we love them.

We're to give warnings, but we also need to willingly receive them. The fact is we all have "blind spots." We often use this phrase to describe a driver's inability to see certain areas around the vehicle he or she is driving. In order to see the "blind spot," the driver needs a little help from someone else in the passenger seat of the car. This illustration helps explain the foundation of exhortation—we need friends in the car with us to help us see approaching danger. Anyone who would knowingly let us swerve into the path of danger wouldn't be a true friend; and the warning to us is not to tear down our driving skills, but to keep us on the correct path.

As in driving, the warning should be immediate—*"as long as it is called 'today.'"* We should seize the moment because waiting on warning only leads to disaster. It takes a risk to get involved, but how many marriages could have been salvaged, how many relationships healed, how many bad decisions averted, if someone had loved enough to warn?

As you think of your Christian friends or small group, is there someone who needs to be warned? Perhaps you see a pattern developing in someone's life that is unhealthy. Maybe you have noticed an increasing cynicism, or a flirtation, or mounting financial debt, or workaholism.

It's likely you'll hear this little voice saying to you, "This is none of your business. Who are you to warn somebody else? You have your own problems." But it is your business. If you don't show up in your friend's life, who will?

POINT TO PONDER:
It is your business!

VERSE TO REMEMBER:
"You must warn each other every day, as long as it is called 'today,'
so that none of you will be deceived by sin and hardened against God."
Hebrews 3:13 (NLT)

QUESTION TO CONSIDER:
We wouldn't hesitate to stop a friend from stepping into traffic.
Why are we hesitant to stop a friend from stepping into sin?

Day 25 Journal

BY GIVING PREFERENCE TO EACH OTHER

Day 26

"Nothing is to be done out of jealousy or vanity; instead, out of humility of mind everyone should give preference to others."
(Philippians 2:3, NJB)

Let others go first.

If you've read *The Purpose Driven® Life*, you'll recall the opening sentence of the book: "It's not about you." God designed us to get outside of ourselves and live on purpose for others. According to Jesus, we live life his way when we give preference to one another: *"Self-help is no help at all. Self-sacrifice is the way, my way, to finding yourself, your true self"* (Matthew 16:25, Msg).

It may be easy to let others go first when you tie with them in the race for the check-out line, but what about weightier matters—the things that are really important to you? Sometimes showing preference to others means sacrificing for what is best for the Body of Christ. We're in community, and we say "we" instead of "I" and "our" instead of "mine." The Bible says, *"Don't think only of your own good. Think of other Christians and what is best for them"* (1 Corinthians 10:24, NLT).

The Bible tells us to let others go first, voluntarily placing ourselves in the supportive position on the back-up bench—*"playing second fiddle"* (Romans 12:10, Msg). In order to do this, we have to change the way we think; we must overhaul our perspective. Every day we're taught, encouraged, and lured toward self-centered lives, but Paul challenges us to consider others better than ourselves *"and look out for one another's interests,"* not just our own *(Philippians 2:3-4, TEV).*

Changing our perspective requires that we:

- Diffuse competition. Is there unhealthy competition going on in any of your relationships? Do you try to always "best" others?

- Eliminate pride. Do you want your way all the time? Do you readily admit it when you're wrong? Teenagers, is it possible that your parents might be right? Parents, is it possible that your kids have a valid point?

- Increase consideration. Are you considerate to those around you? Do you assume you have a right to certain things? Are you sensitive to the physical and emotional needs of your spouse?

Giving preference to one another is a monumental challenge, and that's why we must rely on the power of Christ to help us do it. Paul hints at this in *Ephesians 5:21 (NIV)*, where he says, *"Submit to one another out of reverence for Christ."* It is out of respect for Christ that we find the strength to put others first. When we truly respect Christ, it shows up in our willingness to submit to others and to put them first.

Our changing perspective will quickly begin to show up in our behavior, such as when we:

- Let someone share their story without trying to top it.
- Let someone else choose the restaurant.
- Listen with interest and attention.
- Let someone else take the credit.
- Genuinely celebrate other people's victories.
- Serve our small group with no hidden agenda.
- Pray fervently and consistently for a need in someone's life.

As you journal today, make a list of five specific ways in which you can show preference to your family or the members of your small group. You'll discover an incredible joy in this "preferential" lifestyle, as you find it truly is *"more blessed to give than to receive" (Acts 20:35, NIV).*

POINT TO PONDER:
Let others go first.

VERSE TO REMEMBER:
"... out of humility of mind everyone should give preference to others."
Philippians 2:3b (NJB)

QUESTION TO CONSIDER:
In what ways and situations do you need to "practice playing second fiddle" this week?

3-23-06

Day 26 Journal

BY CONFESSING TO EACH OTHER

"Confess your sins to each other and pray for each other so that you may be healed. The prayer of a righteous man is powerful and effective."
James 5:16 (NIV)

The purpose of confession is not disgrace, but grace.

When the Bible uses the word confess, it literally means "to say the same." When we confess, we are saying the same about our sin that God says. It means we acknowledge and take responsibility for our sin. We confess because of a repentant heart that desires to obey and please God, not merely because we got caught doing something wrong.

So, to whom do we confess? Do we confess to Jesus or to people? The answer is "yes." The Bible teaches we should confess to both. The Apostle John wrote, *"But if we confess our sins to him, he is faithful and just to forgive us and to cleanse us from every wrong" (1 John 1:9, NLT).* Scripture is clear that only Christ can forgive our sins and that as Christians we can go to him anytime, anyplace, and he will forgive us.

It's also important to note that this forgiveness has to do with fellowship, not sonship. John was writing to believers about what believers do when they sin. In other words, you don't need to confess your sin to get back into God's family—you're still a family member—you confess to restore your fellowship with God.

We're also to confess our sins to others: *"Confess your sins to each other and pray for each other so that you may be healed. The prayer of a righteous man is powerful and effective" (James 5:16, NIV).* Notice that James says our confession to each other is *"so that you may be healed,"* not that you may be forgiven. Forgiveness only comes from God, but healing comes from confession in community. The confession James speaks of is not the result of interrogation, it is the result of a contrite heart that voluntarily acknowledges sin. *"When you are guilty, immediately confess the sin that you've committed" (Leviticus 5:5, Msg).*

So, where in the church could this ever happen? Most confession won't and shouldn't take place in a corporate worship service. It is not likely to happen in the typical Sunday school class where the focus is usually on Bible study. The one place in church life where James 5:16 has the best shot at being practiced is in a small group. It must be in an environment that is safe and marked by unconditional love.

Confession and confidentiality go hand in hand. People must be able to trust that if they share, their confession won't go any further. Also, the group must be a place of grace. There should never be a question of whether or not people will be loved and accepted, no matter what they share.

Why does God want us to confess to each other? There are at least two powerful reasons.

First, it is one thing to read of God's forgiveness in the Bible, but it is quite another thing to hear and feel God's grace and love in the voices of your friends. When we confess, and then are still unconditionally embraced by our small group, God's love and forgiveness become more tangible.

Second, confession reduces the power of a secret. The beginning of healing is revealing. There is something cleansing and liberating about coming clean through confession. It also allows our group to come alongside us to support and pray for us in our struggle. The purpose of confession is not disgrace, but grace. The purpose of confession is not humiliation, but restoration.

Finally, what should we do when someone confesses to us?

- Listen with tenderness.
- Don't try to minimize the seriousness of their sin.
- Don't try to fix anything.
- Be emotionally present in the moment and hurt with them.
- Affirm your love and God's forgiveness.
- Ask, "How can we support you?"
- Pray for and with them.

This whole idea of confession may seem foreign and awkward. But it is biblical and important for your spiritual health. Is God speaking to you at this very moment about some hidden area of your life that needs to be confessed?

POINT TO PONDER:
The purpose of confession is not disgrace, but grace.

VERSE TO REMEMBER:
"Confess your sins to each other and pray for each other so that you may be healed. The prayer of a righteous man is powerful and effective."
James 5:16 (NIV)

QUESTION TO CONSIDER:
If God is speaking to you about a hidden area of your life that needs to be confessed, what are you going to do about it?

Day 27 Journal

BY FORGIVING EACH OTHER

"Be kind and compassionate to one another, forgiving each other,
just as in Christ God forgave you."
Ephesians 4:32 (NIV)

Fellowship without forgiveness is impossible.

As believers, we're called *"to settle our relationships with each other"* (2 Corinthians 5:18, Msg). We need to consistently forgive others and receive forgiveness from others, or we'll *"give up in despair"* (2 Corinthians 2:7, CEV).

Whenever we're hurt by someone, we must make a choice: will we focus on retaliation or on resolution?

The Bible speaks candidly about settling the score: *"Make sure that nobody pays back wrong for wrong, but always try to be kind to each other and to everyone else"* (1 Thessalonians 5:15, NIV). In God's economy, it's not enough to say we won't seek revenge; we're to press into the very heart of forgiveness—*"forgiving each other, just as in Christ God forgave you"* (Ephesians 4:32, NIV).

As you read the Bible, it becomes very clear that forgiveness is not optional for the Christ-follower. God sets the standard so high because he knows how much is at stake in your life. Bitterness and unforgiveness are a cancer that will eventually destroy you from the inside out. Forgiveness is the scalpel that removes the tumor of bitterness. This doesn't mean you'll always be able to forgive and be done with it. You may have to keep forgiving again and again until you know you've released the offender. But forgiveness is a choice you can make and one that God expects.

In the book of Colossians, Paul provides the basis and motivation for forgiveness: *"You must make allowance for each other's faults and forgive the person who offends you. Remember, the Lord forgave you, so you must forgive others"* (Colossians 3:13, NLT). And *Romans 5:8 (NIV)* tells us that *"while we were still sinners,"* (before we apologized) *"Christ died for us."* When we remember the price Jesus paid to forgive us, how can we not forgive?

So what does it mean to forgive? First, let's agree it doesn't mean doing some sort of mental gymnastics to erase your hurt, and it doesn't mean pretending that you weren't hurt. Rather, forgiveness means you no longer hold the offense against the offender. It means you've pardoned the debt and you've intentionally chosen to release the one who hurt you. You love deeply, *"because love covers over a multitude of sins"* (1 Peter 4:8, NIV).

Here are some steps toward forgiveness:

- Talk to God before talking to the person. Like David in the Psalms, use prayer to ventilate vertically. Cry out to God, telling him exactly how you feel. He won't be surprised or upset by your anger, hurt, insecurity, or bitterness.

- Always take the initiative. It doesn't matter whether you are the offender or the offended; Jesus told us to make the first move. *"This is how I want you to conduct yourself in these matters. If you enter your place of worship and, about to make an offering, you suddenly remember a grudge a friend has against you, abandon your offering, leave immediately, go to this friend and make things right. Then and only then, come back and work things out with God"* (Matthew 5:23-24, Msg).

- Confess your part of the conflict. If you're serious about restoring a relationship, you should begin with admitting your own mistakes or sin. Jesus said it's the way to see things more clearly: *"First get rid of the log from your own eye; then perhaps you will see well enough to deal with the speck in your friend's eye" (Matthew 7:5, NLT).*

Maybe you need to stop right now and have an honest conversation with God about someone you need to forgive. Your heavenly Father knows that it's not easy to let go of your hurts. But he will help you and give you the grace to forgive. So do it NOW. You'll be glad you did.

POINT TO PONDER:
Fellowship without forgiveness is impossible.

VERSE TO REMEMBER:
*"Be kind and compassionate to one another,
forgiving each other, just as in Christ God forgave you."
Ephesians 4:32 (NIV)*

QUESTIONS TO CONSIDER:
If there's someone you need to forgive, when are you going to do it? If there is someone you've wronged, when are you going to ask for forgiveness?

Day 28 Journal

BY BEING WILLING TO SERVE

"You, my brothers, were called to be free. But do not use your freedom to indulge the sinful nature; rather, serve one another in love."
Galatians 5:13 (NIV)

We are saved to serve each other.

Many people have the misconception that being "called" by God is something that only missionaries, pastors, nuns, and other church leaders experience. But the Bible says that everyone is called to serve God by serving others. We are not saved *by* serving, but we are saved *for* serving.

Today's verse gives us three insights about serving God by serving each other:

First, the basis for serving others is salvation. Paul says, *"You were called to be free."* You cannot serve God until you've been set free by Jesus. It's the prerequisite for serving. Until you experience the transforming power of God's grace in your life, you're too enslaved by your own habits, hurts, and hang-ups to think much about others. Without the freedom of forgiveness, you'll end up serving for the wrong reasons: trying to earn the approval of others, trying to run away from your pain, trying to remedy your guilt, trying to impress God. Service that's motivated by these illegitimate reasons is bound to leave you burned out and bitter in the end.

Second, the barrier to serving others is selfishness. Paul warns, *"Do not use your freedom to indulge the sinful nature."* The #1 reason we don't have the time or energy to serve others is because we're preoccupied with our own agendas, dreams, and pleasures. In the late 1960s, the "hippie" movement swept through San Francisco and then the nation. Hippies were mostly college-age young adults who rebelled against authority and flaunted their freedom by indulging in free sex and free drugs. They slept in Golden Gate Park and panhandled instead of getting jobs.

They proudly labeled themselves "the counter-culture," yet they did exactly what most people in our culture do: they indulged themselves. Even today, television commercials scream: "Obey your thirst! Have it your way! Do what's best for you. Look out for #1." Most of the time, we're more interested in "serve-us" than service.

Yet, it is in serving others that we adopt a true counter-cultural lifestyle. It is far more radical to look out for someone else's needs than it is to look out for yourself. Only a small minority of people use their lives to serve others. But Jesus said, *"If you insist on saving your life, you will lose it. Only those who throw away their lives for my sake and for the sake of the Good News will ever know what it means to really live"* (Mark 8:35, LB).

✳ Third, the motive for serving is love. Paul says, *"Serve one another in love."* This is an important key to building community. Without love, service doesn't count in God's eyes. *1 Corinthians 13:3 (Msg.)* says, *"No matter what I say, what I believe, and what I do, I'm bankrupt without love."* God is far more interested in why you serve others than he is interested in how well you serve them. He's always looking at your heart.

This week, we'll look at six more "one anothers"—practical ways your small group can serve each other and the rest of your church family together. But today is the time to prepare your heart for these lessons. Don't view serving others as an obligation or a duty. Serve willingly and eagerly out of love for Jesus and gratitude for all he's done for you.

Then remember that serving on earth is practice for eternity, and you are most like Jesus when you are serving others. After washing his disciples' feet, Jesus said, *"I have given you an example to follow. Do as I have done to you"* (John 13:14-15, NLT).

POINT TO PONDER:
We're saved to serve each other.

VERSE TO REMEMBER:
"Each one of us needs to look after the good of the people around us, asking ourselves, 'How can I help?'"
Romans 15:2 (Msg.)

QUESTION TO CONSIDER:
How will you serve someone in your church or small group today?

Day 29 Journal

BY HELPING EACH OTHER

"By helping each other with your troubles, you truly obey the law of Christ."
Galatians 6:2 (NCV)

We're to carry each other's burdens.

The sense of this verse is that we're to help our brothers and sisters carry the heavy burdens of life—a terrible loss, a crushing circumstance, a painful diagnosis. These are the kinds of troubles that threaten to overwhelm and destroy us, similar to the pressing weight of the cross that Jesus carried to Golgotha *(John 19:17)*.

Like Simon from Cyrene, who shouldered the heavy wooden cross with Jesus *(Mark 15:21)*, we're to step in with support for our friends, even if that means we carry their burden for a while. Martin Luther referred to this as the law of mutual love; as a community of believers, we are to work together to face life's many challenges *(Galatians 6:2)*.

Our acts of love and support for one another complete this *"law of Christ."* We're better together as we help each other face the troubles in our homes, our careers, our marriages, and with our health. We build our lives on the promise of the Father, who will never leave or forsake us *(Deuteronomy 31:6, NIV)*, and we offer that same promise to our families and friends.

Here are some foundational principles for facing hardships together:

- Open your hearts to God. We feel all sorts of emotions when we face a crisis: fear, anger, worry, depression, resentment, helplessness. Our small groups can be a powerful setting as we pour out our hearts to God (*Psalm 62:8*) and each other. *"The Lord is close to the brokenhearted and saves those who are crushed in spirit"* (*Psalm 34:18, NIV*). Jesus said, *"Blessed are those who mourn, for they will be comforted"* (*Matthew 5:4, NIV*).

- Help others receive as they grieve. Don't allow your small group members to isolate themselves when they're going through a crisis. Offer them support, encouragement, and your presence (*Proverbs 18:24*).

- Be grateful together. Encourage each other to stay free from bitterness (*Hebrews 12:15*), remembering to be grateful and focus on what is left—not what is lost.

- Focus on true value. A crisis often helps us clarify our values—revealing what really matters. Jesus told us, *"Life is not measured by how much one owns"* (*Luke 12:15b, NCV*).

- Lean on Jesus. Let Christ bring stability into the crisis. God constantly cares for his children—helping us to face bad news (*Psalm 112:6-7*).

- Listen for God's direction. *"'I know what I am planning for you,' says the Lord. 'I have good plans for you, not plans to hurt you. I will give you hope and a good future'"* (*Jeremiah 29:11, NCV*). *press through*

- Trust God's hand. *"God is our protection and our strength. He always helps in times of trouble. So we will not be afraid even if the earth shakes, or the mountains fall into the sea"* (*Psalm 46:2, NCV*).

Inevitably, the various members of your small group will face a crisis, and when they do, you should see that crisis as if it is your own, offering tangible support and consistent encouragement. One day, you may need the same help to make it through a difficult time.

Working together, we can confidently say, "*We were really crushed and overwhelmed, and feared we would never live through it . . . We saw how powerless we were to help ourselves; but that was good, for then we put everything into the hands of God, who alone could save us . . . And he did help us and [save] us . . . and we expect him to do it again and again*" (2 Corinthians 1:8b-10, LB).

Does this mean we will always have the outcome we pray for? That the Crisis be removed? No

POINT TO PONDER:
We're to carry each other's burdens.

VERSE TO REMEMBER:
"You obey the law of Christ when you offer each other a helping hand."
Galatians 6:2 (CEV)

QUESTION TO CONSIDER:
Who do you know who needs your help to carry their burden today?

Day 30 Journal

_____

_____

_____

_____

_____

_____

_____

_____

_____

_____

_____

_____

_____

_____

_____

_____

BY BEING GENEROUS WITH EACH OTHER

"All the believers met together constantly and shared everything with each other."
Acts 2:44 (LB)

You have more to share than you realize.

The early church understood this; their life together is described in *Acts 2:44 (LB)*: *"All the believers met together constantly and shared everything with each other."* If anyone in the congregation had a need, everyone worked together to meet it. Some believers were led by the Spirit to sell their possessions and give the money to those in need *(Acts 4:34-35)*.

This is not communism; it is commonness. It means admitting that keeping more than we could possibly need is *"not doing right" (2 Kings 7:8-9, NIV)*, and that we should *"be generous with the different things God gave [us], passing them around so all get in on it" (1 Peter 4:10, Msg)*. Everything we have is a *"good and perfect gift" (James 1:17, NIV)* from our Heavenly Father, who lavishes on us *"every spiritual blessing in the heavenly realms because we belong to Christ"* *(Ephesians 1:3, NLT)*. We give generously because God gave generously to us.

You may not have a lot of money to give, but you can give your time and talents; that's a major part of being generous. But you can also be generous with your abundance of possessions. For example:

- Baby clothes stored in a closet
- An old computer
- Extra tickets to a sporting event
- Frequent flyer miles
- The two extra toasters from your wedding

Imagine how much you could bless others if you simply cleaned your closets and passed along your abundance—giving the things you don't use to people who will. When you pass these items on, model unconditional love by giving them with no strings attached.

But here's an important point: you don't have to give something away to share it! You may be rich in the sense that you have lots of things you can loan to others. Anyone can afford to share such things as:

- Your garage full of tools
- Your empty vacation cabin
- Your rarely used extra car

When we don't share, we're keeping the community of believers from experiencing the full blessings of God, and we're being poor stewards of all God has given us. It means some gifts from God are not used as extensively as they could be. Most of all, we're robbing ourselves of the joy of generous living among Christian brothers and sisters.

There's another reason we need to learn to be generous with one another: it will build our faith towards being generous with the world. About three billion people, roughly half the world, live on less than $2 a day. Your small group could re-shape the lives of an entire village in a Third World country by living generously together. The lawn mower you loan to another believer or the baby clothes you pass on to another family could help your group collectively save enough money to support a Third World village for more than a month!

As we learn to be generous together, here are some characteristics to develop:

- Remember it all belongs to God. Our harvest comes from God, who even gave us the seeds to grow the crop: *"He gives you something you can then*

give away, which grows into full-formed lives, robust in God"
(2 Corinthians 9:10, Msg).

• Give with a cheerful heart. God doesn't want your possessions; he wants your heart *(Matthew 6:21)*. What motivates your giving? Paul wrote, *"God loves a cheerful giver" (2 Corinthians 9:7b, NIV).*

• Never give under pressure. God wants you to *"make up your own mind what you will give."* This will *"protect you against sob stories and arm-twisting" (2 Corinthians 9:7, Msg)*. If you feel pressured to give, don't. God wants you to carefully consider your generosity, and to then give voluntarily. Be sensitive to those in your small group as they decide what God would have them give and share.

You really do have more to share than you realize. And the Bible promises, *"A generous man will prosper; he who refreshes others will himself be refreshed" (Proverbs 11:25, NIV)*. Learn to live generously. You'll be richer for it in the end.

POINT TO PONDER:
You have more to share than you realize.

VERSE TO REMEMBER:
"... make up your own mind what you will give ...
God loves it when the giver delights in the giving."
2 Corinthians 9:7 (Msg.)

QUESTION TO CONSIDER:
How attached are you to your possessions—
do you own them or do they own you?

Day 31 Journal

BY BEING HUMBLE WITH EACH OTHER

"All of you, serve each other in humility, for God sets himself against the proud, but he shows favor to the humble."

1 Peter 5:5 (NLT)

Remember to be forgetful.

The life of a servant requires a kind of forgetfulness, the ability to forget ourselves *"long enough to lend a helping hand" (Philippians 2:4b, Msg)*. We're to develop an attitude like Jesus, *"who, being in very nature God"* voluntarily took the *"nature of a servant" (Philippians 2:6-7, NIV)*, and then we're to *"look after the good of the people around us, asking ourselves, 'How can I help?'" (Romans 15:2, Msg)*.

One night Jesus answered this question about help when he *"stood up and took off his outer clothing. Taking a towel, he wrapped it around his waist. Then he poured water into a bowl and began to wash the followers' feet, drying them with the towel that was wrapped around him" (John 13:4-5, NCV)*. Washing another's feet was typically a task reserved for the lowliest of servants; but Jesus, speaking without words, showed us that no act of service was beneath his heart of love. He placed the needs of his disciples above his own, even as the shadow of his death darkened the Upper Room.

The key to humility is knowing who you are; when you understand who you are, you're comfortable grabbing the towel instead of the spotlight. Jesus didn't care if someone mistook him for a servant because he knew it was his mission in life. He was more interested in serving others than he was in impressing others.

The centurion in Luke 7 was a man of noteworthy humility. With Jesus on the way, the commander sent a message: *"Lord, don't trouble yourself, for I do not deserve to have you come under my roof . . . Say the word, and my servant will be healed. For I myself am a man under authority, with soldiers under me. I tell this one, 'Go,' and he goes; and that one, 'Come,' and he comes"* (Luke 7:5-8, NIV).

He could have insisted Jesus complete the journey to his home. And wouldn't that have put him in the community's spotlight? But the need was for his servant to be healed, not to impress the countryside.

Even more remarkable is the way the soldier describes himself to Jesus. Instead of emphasizing his high rank, he notes his proper place under authority. He understood that his authority to give orders was interconnected with his ability to receive them, and that his value and worth had nothing to do with his position in the pecking order.

Humility simply means we hold an accurate and unbiased assessment of our strengths and weaknesses. We understand our shape and our gifts, and we're aware of, but not fretting over, our limitations. We see everything we have as a gift from God, and we know that without him we have nothing.

Our critical first step toward developing humility like Jesus is to fully grasp the magnitude of God's love for us. As we let the length, width, depth, and height of his love seep into our innermost parts *(Ephesians 3:18)*, we'll find our insecurities washed away, and we'll be empowered to serve others in authentic humility.

Our second step is to surrender our agenda to God. We pray, "God, I'm going with your plans for my life, not my own. I've got plans, I've got dreams, I've got goals, I've got ambitions, but I know that you put me on this earth for a reason, for a purpose, and I am intentionally choosing your plan for my life instead of my own. I know you're not going to reveal it to me all at once; it's going to come a little bit at a time. But, I'm willing to take it one step at a time, knowing your plan is better than mine."

Jesus didn't care if someone mistook him for a servant—how about you?

POINT TO PONDER:
Humility is the result of knowing who you are.

VERSE TO REMEMBER:
"Serve each other in humility . . ."
1 Peter 5:5a (NLT)

QUESTION TO CONSIDER:
How do you feel when you're treated like a servant?

Day 32 Journal

BY USING OUR TALENTS TO BLESS EACH OTHER

Day 33

*"Each of you has been blessed with one of God's many wonderful gifts
to be used in the service of others. So use your gift well."*
1 Peter 4:10 (CEV)

Find the intersection of God's will and your gifts.

"God has given each of us the ability to do certain things well," wrote the
Apostle Paul *(Romans 12:6-8, NLT)*. Although he is speaking to specific spiritual
gifts in this passage, his point is universal—whatever abilities God gives us, we're
to use for blessing others.

The Bible is full of examples of God's people using the gifts he's given them
to bless others for his glory. This list of gifts includes, but is not limited to:
artistry, architecture, administration, baking, boat making, debating, designing,
embalming, embroidering, engraving, farming, fishing, gardening, leading, man-
aging, masonry, making music, making weapons, needlework, painting, sailing,
selling, being a soldier, tailoring, teaching, writing literature and poetry.

God wants us to use our gifts in *"inventive"* ways *(Hebrews 10:24, Msg)*,
breaking out of the box that limits our concepts of Christian service to a small
list of traditional roles. He wants us to operate from the perspective that whatever
we're gifted to do can be done *"for the glory of God"* (1 Corinthians 10:31, NIV).
He gave you abilities, interests, talents, gifts, your personality, and life experiences for
this very reason. Yet, most of these gifts remain untapped, unrecognized, and unused.

Would it surprise you to know that some studies indicate the average believer
possesses between 500 to 700 different skills and abilities—all gifts meant to

make a contribution to the Body of Christ? You needn't be concerned if some of your talents seem quite ordinary; they're still eternally important to God. Jesus said, *"If you give even a cup of cold water to one of the least of my followers, you will surely be rewarded"* (Matthew 10:42, NLT).

Like stained glass, our different personalities reflect God's light in a variety of colors and patterns. He shaped us so there would be no duplication—so none of us would have the exact same mix of factors that make us unique. This means no one else on earth will ever be able to do the things for others that you are able to do. *"It is God himself who has made us what we are and given us new lives from Christ Jesus; and long ages ago he planned that we should spend these lives in helping others"* (Ephesians 2:10, LB).

One way to assess your gifts and abilities is to look at your S.H.A.P.E., an acrostic to help you assess God's design in your life:

- Spiritual Gifts: God gives you spiritual gifts to use in ministry *(1 Corinthians 12, Romans 12, Ephesians 4)*.

- Heart: Your heart determines why you say the things you do, why you feel the way you do, and why you act the way you do *(Proverbs 4:23, Matthew 12:34)*.

- Abilities: These are natural talents God gives you in order to accomplish his purposes. *Exodus 31:3 (NIV)* states God gives *"skill, ability, and knowledge in all kinds of crafts."*

- Personality: Your personality affects the use of your gifts. For instance, two people may have the gift of evangelism, but if one is introverted and the other is extroverted, that gift will be expressed differently.

- Experiences: These five areas of experience will influence your service to others: educational, vocational, spiritual experiences, ministry, and painful experiences.

It feels good to do what God made you to do and to use your talents to bless others. Phil Vischer, the creator of Veggie Tales and voice of Bob the Tomato, once said, "There is no happier place than the intersection of God's will and your giftedness."

Here are some questions to help you at the intersection:
- What am I good at that I can offer as a ministry to other people?
- What do I know that I can teach to others?
- What can I make and give to someone as a blessing?

Ask the members of your small group to help you determine the things you do best and how they may be used in ministry.

POINT TO PONDER:
Find the intersection of God's will and your gifts.

VERSE TO REMEMBER:
"Let's see how inventive we can be in encouraging love and helping out."
Hebrews 10:24 (Msg.)

QUESTION TO CONSIDER:
How can you use your abilities to serve God by serving others?

Day 33 Journal

BY SACRIFICING FOR EACH OTHER

Day 34

*"We understand what love is when we realize that Christ gave his life for us.
That means we must give our lives for other believers."*
1 John 3:16 (GW)

Serious service requires serious sacrifice.

Yet some believers live lifestyles that require little or no sacrifice. They're familiar with *John 3:16 (NIV)*, *"For God so loved the world . . . ,"* but they need to be equally familiar with *1 John 3:16 (Msg)*: *"This is how we've come to understand and experience love: Christ sacrificed his life for us. This is why we ought to live sacrificially for our fellow believers, and not just be out for ourselves."*

The Apostle Paul says our work as God's servants gets validated when we give during *"hard times, tough times, bad times; when we're beaten up, jailed, and mobbed; working hard, working late, working without eating; with pure hearts, clear heads, steady hands; in gentleness, holiness, and honest love; when we're telling the truth, and when God's showing his power; when we're doing our best setting things right; when we're praised, and when we're blamed; slandered, and honored; true to our word, though distrusted; ignored by the world, but recognized by God; terrifically alive, though rumored to be dead; beaten within an inch of our lives, but refusing to die; immersed in tears, yet always filled with deep joy; living on handouts, yet enriching many; having nothing, having it all"* (2 Corinthians 6:4-10, Msg).

Whatever it cost to enrich the lives of others on behalf of Christ, Paul considered it a worthwhile sacrifice *(Philippians 3:7)*. He kept his eyes firmly fixed on the prize *(Philippians 3:14)*. He followed Jesus, who *"could put up with*

anything along the way: cross, shame, whatever" (Hebrews 12:2, Msg). Jesus set aside the privileges of deity and took on the "status of a slave" (Philippians 2:7, Msg), so that those who believed in him could be "signed, sealed, and delivered by the Holy Spirit" (Ephesians 1:13, Msg).

You and I benefit daily from the sacrifices of other believers. One simple illustration is the building where you meet for your weekly worship service. Have you ever considered how many people have sacrificed so you would have a place of worship?

Generations before us have sacrificed on our behalf, and now it's our turn to serve God's purpose in our generation (Acts 13:36). God doesn't ask us to give any more than Jesus, who came "as a sacrifice to clear away our sins and the damage they've done to our relationship with God . . . if God loved us like this, we certainly ought to love each other" (1 John 4:10-11, Msg).

Our Christlike sacrifice should be:

* • Voluntary. Jesus said his life was not taken from him, but given freely (John 10:18). Likewise, the first Christian martyr, Stephen, offered up his life voluntarily (Acts 7:59-60). We may not be asked to die for our faith, but Jesus does expect us to die daily to our self-interests for the sake of others (Luke 9:23).

* • Costly. Israel's King David said he would offer no sacrifice to God that cost him nothing (2 Samuel 24:24). Serving God is costly, and the cost is more than just financial. We may be asked to give up our dreams, our expectations, our reputations, our retirements—whatever God asks of us in order to enrich others.

• Steady. We're to pour ourselves *"out for each other in acts of love"* (*Ephesians 4:2, Msg.*), doing for others what they cannot do for themselves; we're to do this consistently, and not in *"fits and starts"* (*Ephesians 4:2, Msg*).

What are some ways to sacrifice daily?

• Give your time to care for those around you.

• Give your reputation by standing for Jesus.

• Risk rejection by defending another believer.

• Support people in your small group who want to go on a mission.

• Use your vacation in order to do ministry.

When we willingly follow the command of Scripture to *"offer your bodies as living sacrifices"* (*Romans 12:1, NIV*), we discover that serving each other is the central aspect of God's *"good, pleasing, and perfect will"* for our lives (*Romans 12:2, NIV*).

 POINT TO PONDER:
Serious service requires serious sacrifice.

VERSE TO REMEMBER:
"…we must give our lives for other believers."
1 John 3:16b (GW)

QUESTION TO CONSIDER:
What sacrifice can you make that will enrich the lives of many?

1-9-05

This day of the journey has had the biggest impact. I have begun taking Communion daily for about a week now. The Holy Spirit has been revealing deeper understanding regarding the reason to take Communion. Wine/blood/lifeforce and bread/nourishment/spiritual and physical needs are met. Also red/blood white/bread represent the need to unite the masculine and feminine principles: submission/feminine/Mary/emotions/ (choice) heart with masculine/assertiveness/ "bridging force"/Jesus/mind to bring under the will of the Holy Spirit. Symbols and meanings from "Cloud Nine"

BY COOPERATING WITH EACH OTHER

"We work together as partners who belong to God."

1 Corinthians 3:9a (NLT)

We are better together.

God's plan is for us to partner with him and partner with each other to fulfill his purposes. But the thing about partnerships is they're made from parts. As we learned in Day 15, *"We are all parts of his one body, and each of us has different work to do. And since we are all one body in Christ, we belong to each other, and each of us needs all the others" (Romans 12:5, NLT).*

We've learned God wants unity in community—a oneness of spirit where we agree *"wholeheartedly with each other, loving one another, and working together with one heart and purpose" (Philippians 2:2, NLT).* Our diversity is a significant aspect of God's blueprint to create this unity. We are all together as Christ's body, each of us a *"separate and necessary part . . ." (1 Corinthians 12:27, NLT).*

We see this modeled every weekend at Saddleback Church as people with different talents and abilities come together to prepare the campus for our worship services. Some people are cleaning, others are organizing; some people are preparing to teach, others to greet—all individuals combined as one Body to tell others about Jesus. And we're just one congregation—other parts of the Body are doing similar work around the world.

It is a paradox of our faith that we find our unique and specific purpose in life only after we yield our individualism for the good of many. We become one heart and mind with God and with other believers *(John 17:21-22)*, and in the safety of that community, our true value as individuals will emerge.

Together, we enter into a desperate partnership, with a task so large—telling the world that God sent Jesus *(John 17:21)*—we can't possibly do it alone or without God. *"We take our lead from Christ, who is the source of everything we do. He keeps us in step with each other. His very breath and blood flow through us, nourishing us so that we will grow up healthy in God, robust in love"* (Ephesians 4:15b-16, Msg).

We are better together; and this 40 Day study is meant to help us see our connectedness, and to encourage us to start working together as a community of interdependent partners. The people in your small group have not come together by accident; surely the hand of God assembled you for *"such a time as this"* (Esther 4:14, NIV), with the necessary parts for you to collectively learn to love, fellowship, grow, serve, be on mission, and worship together.

This week in your small group, identify where each member is strong, affirming and confirming each other's shape. This is an important step in working together on your ministry project.

As you journal today, think about your place in the Body of Christ—within your small group and congregation.

One application note: Plan a day when your group works with the other small groups in the congregation for a church cleaning day. Walk through your campus as if you were a visitor, and make any adjustments you see necessary.

POINT TO PONDER:
We are better together.

VERSE TO REMEMBER:
"We work together as partners who belong to God."
1 Corinthians 3:9a (NLT)

QUESTION TO CONSIDER:
How do your gifts and abilities complement the others in your group?

Day 35 Journal

BY WORSHIPING WEEKLY

"You have six days to do your work,
but the seventh day of each week is holy because it belongs to me."
Leviticus 23:3 (CEV)

There is a rhythm to life.

Did you know that God commands that you take an entire day off every week? God considers it so important that he included it in his "top ten" list of rules for living—the Ten Commandments. It's # 4, right along with don't murder, don't commit adultery, and don't steal! That's how serious God considers this issue.

The Bible calls it the Sabbath, a complete day set aside for rest and corporate worship. Not for errands. Not for catching up on unfinished work. Not for planning other meetings. It's for rest and corporate worship, and it's not optional. If you aren't taking a weekly Sabbath, you're breaking one of the Ten Commandments every week.

Why is a weekly Sabbath so important? Jesus explained, *"The Sabbath was made for man, not man for the Sabbath" (Mark 2:27, NIV).* Jesus knew that two of your greatest needs on a weekly basis are rest and worship with other believers. It's part of God's planned rhythm of life.

But with today's fast-paced lifestyles, Saturdays and Sundays are often busier than the rest of the week. We cram all the activities we possibly can into the weekends so that when Monday rolls around we've neither rested nor have we worshiped.

For many, worshiping with others is a last alternative, something they do only when it's convenient and doesn't interfere with other plans. Others say, "I worship when I'm out in nature, camping or water skiing." But that's not the kind of worship God commands once a week. It is to be corporate worship together with other believers; God wants us to gather with the rest of his family to praise him together. When we do, he meets us there. Jesus said, *"Whenever two or three of you come together in my name, I am there with you" (Matthew 18:20, CEV).*

In corporate worship, we worship in ways we are unable to by ourselves. As we sing and celebrate together, pray and confess together, share and meditate together, give offerings and commit together, our faith is reaffirmed, our hope is reinforced, and our love is renewed. That can only happen in community.

This week we'll look at ways we can deepen our worship together, but let me challenge you today to take God's command seriously. If you tend to be a workaholic, and you never really let down and rest, or if your commitment to weekly worship is casual, based on convenience rather than commitment, you need to put a Sabbath day in your schedule. Memorize today's Bible verse to help you remember the rhythm of a balanced, healthy life. And sit with your small group this weekend on Celebration Sunday.

"Let us not give up the habit of meeting together, as some are doing. Instead, let us encourage one another all the more, since you see that the Day of the Lord is coming nearer" (Hebrews 10:25, TEV).

POINT TO PONDER:

The Sabbath is a time to *"Be still and know that I am God" (Psalm 46:10, NIV).*

VERSE TO REMEMBER:

*"You have six days when you can do your work,
but the seventh day of each week is holy because it belongs to me."
Leviticus 23:3a, (CEV)*

QUESTION TO CONSIDER:

What do you need to work on to get your schedule
and priorities in step with God's rhythm?

Day 36 Journal

BY PREPARING FOR WORSHIP

Day 37

"(Rehoboam) did evil, because he did not prepare his heart to seek the Lord."
2 Chronicles 12:14 (NKJV)

When we worship with an unprepared heart, we sin.

God doesn't expect our corporate worship to be perfect, but he does expect it to be focused, with each of us arriving for the service with a prepared heart and uncluttered mind. In this corporate offering to God, we're to enter his presence—the presence of a holy being, the one and only true God—with thanksgiving *(Psalm 95:2)*.

Our corporate worship is really an extension of our daily walk with God, where our attitudes and actions already serve to worship our Creator *(Romans 12)*. Our love for each other is another form of worship that becomes a critical element in our ability to *"join together with one voice, giving praise and glory to God" (Romans 15:5-6, NLT)*. If we fail to apply the *"one another"* lessons we've been studying for the past six weeks, we may hinder our congregation's ability to praise God in a unified voice.

We must cleanse ourselves of anything that dampens our fellowship with God. The psalmist declared, *"Who may climb the mountain of the Lord? Who may stand in his holy place? Only those whose hands and hearts are pure, who do not worship idols and never tell lies . . . They alone may enter God's presence and worship the God of Israel" (Psalms 24:3-4, 6, NLT)*. Our hands and hearts have been made pure through the death and resurrection of our Savior, Jesus Christ. It is only through him that our worship is acceptable to God. *"Through Jesus, therefore, let us continually offer a sacrifice of praise, the fruit of lips that confess his name"* Hebrews 13:15 (NIV).

Preparing for worship means we slow down, turn away from ourselves, and begin meditating on what God has done for us. This will fill our hearts with gratitude that we can express through praise: *"I long, yes, I faint with longing to enter the courts of the Lord. With my whole being, body and soul, I will shout joyfully to the living God"* (Psalm 84:2, NLT).

Disharmony within the congregation can also dampen corporate worship. Jesus considered our unity with one another so critical, he said we should stop worship, and go set things right with anyone who is at odds with us. It is only after we have repaired our broken relationships that we should return to worship: *"If you enter your place of worship and, about to make an offering, you suddenly remember a grudge a friend has against you, abandon your offering, leave immediately, go to this friend and make things right. Then and only then, come back and work things out with God"* (Matthew 5:23-24, Msg).

How quickly would broken relationships within the congregation be restored if we all agreed to not have services each weekend until we all were right with one another!

Once we've examined our hearts, we prepare for corporate worship by telling God these three things when we enter the sanctuary for service:

- I'm coming to focus on you, God, not anything else. Help me clear my mind and worship you with an undivided heart. I desire to come wholeheartedly into your presence *(Psalm 86:11).*

- I am coming to give to you, not to receive. I desire to seek your face and not your hand. I have no agenda except to minister to you, my Lord *(Psalm 41:13)*.

- I'm coming to offer my praises and to use my heart, my voice, and my hands to worship you. I choose to focus on your goodness and mercy, and not human error or methodology. I choose not to criticize my brothers and sisters who are also coming to give glory to your name.

God's invitation to come to him in worship is an immeasurable privilege. May we never take it for granted.

POINT TO PONDER:
When we worship with an unprepared heart, we sin.

VERSE TO REMEMBER:
"Who may stand in his holy place? Only those whose hands and hearts are pure."
Psalms 24:3-4, 6 (NLT)

QUESTION TO CONSIDER:
What can you do to prepare yourself for corporate worship this weekend?

Day 37 Journal

BY PRAYING TOGETHER

"They all met together continually for prayer..."
Acts 1:14 (NLT)

God intended our prayer to be a priority, not a postscript.

In many churches and small groups, prayer is like the singing of the national anthem at a sporting event: we wouldn't think of starting without it, but it has little relevance to the main event. Early Christians *"met together continually for prayer . . ." (Acts 1:14, NLT).* The Bible says we're to devote ourselves to prayer, *"being watchful and thankful" (Colossians 4:2, NIV).*

Prayer invites the presence and power of God into our circumstances and into our group life. Most of us know this to be true, yet when it comes to practice, prayer gets marginalized. Many Christians live with a sense of guilt and inadequacy when it comes to their prayer life.

But let's be honest, being devoted to prayer and learning to pray together is not easy. It's interesting that the only time the disciples ever asked Jesus to teach them something was when they said, *"Lord, teach us to pray" (Luke 11:1, NIV).*

Here are four practical suggestions that will energize prayer in your small group:

First, make prayer a priority of your group meeting. In Acts 4 when the apostles were unjustly arrested, imprisoned, and threatened, they didn't call for a protest. They didn't initiate a letter-writing campaign. They didn't use their political clout. Instead, they called a prayer meeting. Soon the place where they were praying was literally shaking with the power of God.

Stop for a moment and consider the fact that the God of the universe wants to hear from you and your small group. *"For what great nation has a god as near to them as the Lord our God is near to us whenever we call on him?"* (Deuteronomy 4:7, NLT). The Bible also says that we can boldly go into his presence knowing that he is a good Father who delights to meet the needs of his kids: *"So let us come boldly to the throne of our gracious God. There we will receive his mercy, and we will find grace to help us when we need it"* (Hebrews 4:16, NLT).

So what would it look like if your group made prayer a priority? This might be a good discussion question for your group. Also, how can you help your group expand their view of prayer?

Second, get everyone to participate in group prayer. There is power in praying for each other but also in praying with each other. If your group is like many, there are likely two or three people who seem to be comfortable praying aloud in a group. So before long it becomes the unspoken expectation that these group members are the designated pray-ers.

If your group is really going to embrace communal prayer, it's important to get everyone involved. If you're someone who doesn't feel comfortable praying in a group, here are some ways to get started:

- Start small. Your first step may not be closing the group meeting in prayer. Your first step might just be a one-sentence prayer.

- Be yourself. You don't need to use a special voice or certain words. Just talk to God like you would talk to a good friend. There is no "right way" to pray.

• Focus on God, not others. After all, you are praying to God.
He cares about your heart, not the eloquence of your words.

Third, share your real needs with the group for prayer. This is one of the great advantages of praying in a small group. In a weekend worship service or prayer meeting with people we don't know, it isn't likely we will share our most personal needs for prayer. However, when we are in a close circle of friends who love us, we are more open to sharing our true needs. It's only when we share specifically that our group can pray specifically—helping us see how God answers specifically.

Fourth, learn to pray "in the moment." When someone shares a need, a crisis, or a praise report, get in the habit of stopping right then and praying together. People's tears are often God's invitation to your group to stop and pray. Sometimes the most important thing you accomplish in your group is tenderly gathering around a person in need and praying on his or her behalf.

Praying together is one of the greatest privileges we have as members of Christ's community. Let's be people who take full advantage of that privilege.

POINT TO PONDER:
As your group prays together, your faith will be strengthened,
and you'll see God's power unleashed.

VERSE TO REMEMBER:
"They all met together continually for prayer . . ."
Acts 1:14 (NLT)

QUESTION TO CONSIDER:
How high a priority is prayer in your group life?

Day 38 Journal

_____

_____

_____

_____

_____

_____

_____

_____

_____

_____

_____

_____

_____

_____

_____

BY GIVING OUR OFFERINGS TOGETHER

Day 39

"Every Sunday each of you must put aside some money,
in proportion to what you have earned . . . for the offering."
1 Corinthians 16:2 (TEV)

Giving back to God is the heart of worship.

It may surprise you to learn that Jesus taught more about money and possessions than he did about heaven or hell. The word "give" is used over 1,500 times in the Bible, more than the words faith, hope, love, or pray. Why? Obviously, God doesn't need our money. He's not poor. But God does want us to become like him, and that will only happen if we learn to be generous. God is a giver—the most generous giver in the universe. Everything you have is a gift from God *(1 Chronicles 29:14)*!

In many churches, the giving of offerings is the low point of the service. It's ignored, tolerated, or openly resented by many. But the Bible teaches that God wants our giving to be a deeply meaningful expression of worship in three dimensions—past, present, and future.

First, my giving expresses my gratitude to God for the past. "Thanks" and "giving" go together. When we give back to God, we express our appreciation to him for all the ways he has blessed us. We're saying, "God, we're grateful for all you've done in our lives, and we love you." That's why you should never give under pressure. God wants your giving to be motivated by gratitude. The Bible says, *"Each man should give what he has decided in his heart to give, not reluctantly or under compulsion, for God loves a cheerful giver"* (2 Corinthians 9:7, NIV). A few verses later it says, *". . . your generosity will result in thanksgiving to God"* (2 Corinthians 9:11, NIV).

Second, my giving expresses my priorities in the present. *". . . The purpose of tithing is to teach you always to put God first in your lives" (Deuteronomy 14:23b, LB).* If you want to know what a person really values, just look at his calendar and checkbook. The way people spend their time and money reveals what is really important to them. It's one thing to claim we love God, but the Bible says our giving tests the sincerity of our love *(2 Corinthians 8:8).* When we give the first part of our income to God, on the first day of the week, it is evidence that God holds first place in our hearts. Jesus said, *"For where your treasure is, there your heart will be also" (Matthew 6:21, NIV).*

Third, my giving expresses my faith in God for the future. God sees my giving as a test of my faith. In *Malachi 3:10 (NIV)* he says, *"Bring the whole tithe into the storehouse (temple) . . . Test me in this . . . and see if I will not throw open the floodgates of heaven and pour out so much blessing that you will not have room enough for it."* God challenges us, saying, "I dare you to trust my promise to take care of you as you put me first in your finances. Will you trust me?" It has always amazed me that many people are willing to trust God for their eternal salvation but won't trust him enough to tithe.

In today's verse, Paul gives us the three characteristics of worshipful giving:

- It is to be weekly: *"Every Sunday . . ."* God wants our giving to be systematic, not spasmodic. Why Sunday? Giving is an act of worship, to be given at the place of worship, when you worship!

- It is to be planned: *"you must put aside some money . . ."* That requires some thought. God doesn't want your giving to be hasty, thoughtless, or impulsive. He wants you to think about what you are giving.

• It is to be proportional: *". . . in proportion to what you have earned."* Tithing is giving 10% of what God has helped you earn. God does not look at the amount you give. He looks at how much you have, and the attitude with which you give it.

As you get ready for this weekend's Celebration Service, ending *40 Days of Community*, consider bringing an offering of thanksgiving to God for all he's done in your life, your small group, and your church during these past six weeks.

POINT TO PONDER:
Giving back to God is the heart of worship.

VERSE TO REMEMBER:
"For where your treasure is, there your heart will be also."
Matthew 6:21 (NIV)

QUESTION TO CONSIDER:
What does my giving say about the direction and condition of my heart?

Day 39 Journal

BY CELEBRATING TOGETHER

*"When you meet together, sing psalms, hymns, and spiritual songs,
as you praise the Lord with all your heart."*
Ephesians 5:19 (CEV)

Worship is a festival, not a funeral!

If anybody on earth has the right to celebrate, it is those of us who've committed our lives to Christ and been accepted into God's family! Just think of all God has done for us!

As we trust in Jesus Christ we are:
- given a new life of purpose and significance!
- forgiven for every sin, mistake, and failure!
- loved unconditionally and accepted by God!
- provided with a spiritual family for our support!
- set free from worry because God is in control!
- offered God's power to overcome hurts, habits, and hang-ups!
- given God's Word with the principles for successful living!
- released from shame, regret, and resentment!
- assured that Satan cannot take away our salvation!
- comforted knowing that "God works all things together for our good!"
- able to face each day with hope and optimistic faith!
- equipped with spiritual gifts, talents, and abilities to use!
- protected by all of God's promises!
- supplied with everything we need!
- guaranteed eternal life in heaven!

If all these benefits don't cause you to celebrate, you need to check your pulse!

It's ironic that in our culture it is acceptable to get excited about anything except God. You can go to a sports event and scream your lungs out, jump up and down, cry, hug, and raise your hands in the air—and people will smile approvingly and call you a "fan." But if you show any joy, heartfelt emotion, or enthusiasm in worship, you're called a "fanatic."

2 Samuel 6:5 (NIV) tells us that *"David and the whole house of Israel were celebrating with all their might before the Lord, with songs and with harps, lyres, tambourines, sistrums and cymbals."* That must have been fun and noisy! But David's wife, Michal, was more concerned about being dignified than celebrating, and she scolded her husband for his enthusiastic worship *(2 Samuel 6:16-20)*. Sadly, the attitude of Michal still hinders many churches today from enjoying worship and fellowship as a community of believers.

God loves to hear his children sing his praises. *Psalm 150:6 (NIV)* says, *"Let everything that has breath praise the Lord."* *Psalm 149:1 (Msg.)* tells us the kind of song to sing: *"Sing to God a brand-new song, praise him in the company of all who love him."* Why a new song? Because God wants to do something fresh in our lives.

The Bible is full of celebrations—feasts and festivals and holidays—because they are important ways to mark progress in our lives. There is great power in remembering. But too often we are so busy moving on to the next activity or task that we don't stop and celebrate what has been accomplished.

As we conclude our *40 Days of Community* this weekend, prepare your heart, and come to church expecting to celebrate with others. Here's your final assignment: Make a list in your journal of all the good things you've seen God do during the past six weeks in your life, in your family, in your small group, and in your church family. Then be prepared to share your list with your small group or with some others on Celebration Sunday this weekend.

Revelation 5:11-13 tells us that heaven is going to be a giant celebration! Let's start practicing our celebration skills now, so our hearts will be ready for heaven! The time we spend singing his praises here on earth will just whet our appetites for the day when the Song will never end.

POINT TO PONDER:
Every time I celebrate God with others, I'm practicing for heaven.

VERSE TO REMEMBER:
"I will celebrate and be joyful because you, Lord, have saved me." Psalm 35:9 (CEV)

QUESTION TO CONSIDER:
When you worship, are you more concerned about what others think or what God thinks?

Day 40 Journal

_____

_____

_____

_____

_____

_____

_____

_____

_____

_____

_____

_____

_____

_____

_____

_____

_____

ONE LAST WORD OF ENCOURAGEMENT:

Let me congratulate you on completing the second of three Purpose Driven® spiritual growth journeys. I urge you to continue having a daily quiet time with God.

If you'd like to receive the free *Purpose Driven® Life* daily devotionals by email, you can sign up at www.purposedrivenlife.com. If you haven't read the books *Purpose Driven® Church* or *Purpose Driven® Life*, I hope you will.

40 DAYS
OF COMMUNITY
study guide

days of
community

You are about to embark on a life-changing experience in your small group. Studying God's Word together always impacts our lives in powerful ways. One of the unique features of this curriculum is that it uses God's five purposes for your life as the format for each session. These purposes, as found in *The Purpose Driven Life*, are Fellowship, Discipleship, Ministry, Mission, and Worship. When you see the following symbols and elements in the study guide, you will know the particular purpose that section promotes. The format of each session is as follows:

Connect Together: Intimate connection with God and his family is the foundation for spiritual growth. This section will help you get to know the members of your group. It will also give you the opportunity to check your progress from week to week.

Grow Together: This section is made up of three components:

• A weekly Bible memory verse that fits the theme of the session.

• A weekly video teaching session by Pastor Rick Warren. Follow along using the outline in this study guide.

• Discussion questions designed to facilitate a deeper understanding of the Bible and to help you consider how the truths of Scripture can impact your life.

Serve Together: Nothing is more fulfilling than using your God-given gifts to serve the needs of others in God's family. This section will help your group discover how you can serve each other and your church together.

Share Together: God wants to use your small group to reach your community for Christ. The Share Together section is designed to give you and your group practical suggestions and exercises for sharing the love of Christ with others.

Worship Together: In each small group session you will have the opportunity to surrender your hearts to God and express your worship to him. In this section you will be led in various forms of small group worship including prayer, Scripture reading, singing together, and sharing what God is doing in your lives. This portion of your session can be very meaningful for your group.

HOST TIPS: These brief instructions in gray type are helpful coaching hints for your group host. Here's your first HOST TIP: The study guide material is meant to be your servant, not your master. So please don't feel you have to answer every question in every section. The point is not to race through the session; the point is to take time to let God work in your lives. Nor is it necessary to "go around the circle" before you move on to the next question. Give people the freedom to speak, but don't insist that they do. Your group will enjoy deeper, more open sharing and discussion if people don't feel pressured to speak up. If your group is unable to work through all the material in a session, we have recommended one question or activity with an asterisk (*) in each section of the study.

HOW TO USE THIS
VIDEO CURRICULUM

Here is a brief explanation of the features on your small group DVD or VHS. These features include six *Helps for Hosts,* one *Group Lifter,* and six *Video Teaching Sessions.* Here's how they work:

Helps for Hosts are special video messages just for group hosts. They provide brief video instruction from Pastor Rick Warren that will help you, the host, prepare for each week's small group session. The group host should watch these features before the group arrives for each study.

The *Group Lifter* is an introductory message to your whole group from Pastor Rick Warren. Be sure to show this *Group Lifter* to your group before you watch the video teaching for session one.

The *Video Teaching Sessions* provide your group with the teaching for each week of the study. Watch these features with your group. After watching the video teaching, continue in your study by working through the discussion questions and activities in the study guide.

Follow these simple steps for a successful small group session:

1) Hosts: Before your group arrives, watch the *"Helps for Hosts"* feature by Pastor Rick Warren. This brief video message will help you prepare for your small group session.

2) Group: Open your group meeting by using the Connect Together section in your study guide.

3) Group: Watch Pastor Rick's video teaching and follow along in the outlines in the study guide.

4) Group: Complete the rest of the discussion materials for each session in the study guide.

It's just that simple. Have a great study together!

SESSION ONE

What matters most

CONNECT TOGETHER . . . . .10 MINUTES

HOST TIP: If your group is unable to work through the entire session, we have recommended one question or activity with an asterisk (*) in each section of the study.

*1. Give everyone a chance to introduce themselves and share why they joined a *40 Days of Community* small group.

2. Open to the *Saddleback Church Group Guidelines* in the *Small Group Resources* section of your workbook, page 231. Take a few minutes to review these group guidelines before you begin this study of *40 Days of Community*. These guidelines will help everyone know how to contribute to a meaningful small group experience.

3. Love is defined in many ways by our culture. How would you define love?

GROW TOGETHER .55 MINUTES

Memory Verse
"Your love for one another will prove to the world that you are my disciples."

John 13:35 (NLT)

Watch the video lesson now and follow along in your outline.

What matters most

"If you are a follower of Christ Jesus…all that matters is your faith that makes you love others." Galatians 5:6 (CEV)

"If I speak in the tongues of men and of angels, but have not love, I am only a resounding gong or a clanging cymbal. [2]If I have the gift of prophecy and can fathom all mysteries and all knowledge, and if I have a faith that can move mountains, but have not love, I am nothing. [3]If I give all I possess to the poor and surrender my body to the flames, but have not love, I gain nothing. [4]Love is patient, love is kind. It does not envy, it does not boast, it is not proud. [5]It is not rude, it is not self-seeking, it is not easily angered, it keeps no record of wrongs. [6]Love does not delight in evil but rejoices with the truth. [7]It always protects, always trusts, always hopes, always perseveres. [8]Love never fails. But where there are prophecies, they will cease; where there are tongues, they will be stilled; where there is knowledge, it will pass away. [9]For we know in part and we prophesy in part, [10]but when perfection comes, the imperfect disappears. [11]When I was a child, I talked like a child, I thought like a child, I reasoned like a child. When I became a man, I put childish ways behind me. [12]Now we see but a poor reflection as in a mirror; then we shall see face to face. Now I know in part; then I shall know fully, even as I am fully known. [13]And now these three remain: faith, hope and love. But the greatest of these is love." 1 Corinthians 13:1-13 (NIV)

Five Radical Statements About Love

If I don't live a life of love:

1. Nothing I ___*say*___ will matter.

   "If I could speak in any language in heaven or on earth, but didn't love others, I would only be making meaningless noise like a loud gong or a clanging cymbal."
   1 Corinthians 13:1 (NLT)

2. Nothing I ___*know*___ will matter.

   "I may have the gift of prophecy. I may understand all the secret things of God and have all knowledge…But if I do not have love, then I am nothing."
   1 Corinthians 13:2 (NCV)

3. Nothing I _believe_ will matter.

"Even if I had the gift of faith so that I could speak to a mountain and make it move, I would still be worth nothing at all without love." 1 Corinthians 13:2b (LB)

4. Nothing I _give_ will matter.

"If I gave everything I have to the poor and even sacrificed my body…but if I didn't love others, I would be of no value whatsoever." 1 Corinthians 13:3 (NLT)

5. Nothing I _accomplish_ will matter.

"No matter what I say, what I believe, or what I do, I'm bankrupt without love." 1 Corinthians 13:3b (Msg.)

What Is Love?

• Love is a _Command_.

"A new command I give you: Love one another. As I have loved you, so you must love one another." John 13:34 (NIV)

• Love is a _choice_.

"Go after a life of love as if your life depended on it—because it does." 1 Corinthians 14:1 (Msg.)

• Love is a _____.

"Let us stop just saying we love people; let us really love them and show it by our actions." 1 John 3:18 (LB)

• Love is a _____.

"God is love. If we keep on loving others, we will stay one in our hearts with God and he will stay one with us." 1 John 4:16b (CEV)

DISCUSSION QUESTIONS

*1. First Corinthians 13:1-3 makes five radical statements about love. They are the first five fill-ins of your outline. Which statement strikes you the most? Why?

2. Second Corinthians 14:1 (Msg.) says, *"Go after a life of love as if your life depended on it—because it does."* On a practical, day-to-day level, what does it mean to "go after a life of love?" What are some steps you can take to live this way?

SERVE TOGETHER .10 MINUTES

*1. One way to "go after" a life of love is to show appreciation to others. Is there a worker in your church who needs to be shown appreciation? As a group, choose either a church staff member or volunteer whom you could affirm this week. You might select an usher, a janitor, a teacher, a secretary, or a youth worker—someone who is involved in serving your congregation. Discuss ways your group can show love and appreciation to that person this week, such as a gift certificate to their favorite store or restaurant, a thank-you card signed by all the members of your group, tickets to a ball game, etc. Recruit one or two volunteers from your group to handle the details. Then, as a group, make plans to present your appreciation gift to the person you chose.

SHARE TOGETHER .15 MINUTES

*1a. Use the *Circles of Life* diagram on page 232 to help you think of a neighbor, family member, friend, or co-worker who would benefit from joining your small group.

1b. Choose a person on your *Circles of Life* diagram to whom you can show the love of Christ this week—someone you have been meaning to call or visit, or someone you need to invite to church. Commit to doing something for that person this week. Tell your small group who the person is and what you will do: send an email, make a call, write a letter, buy a little gift, take him out for coffee, or invite her to join your small group next week.

2. At the end of his message, Pastor Rick asked you to begin discussing a project your whole group can do together to reach out to your community with the love of Christ. Saddleback Church has chosen to respond to the needs of 35,000 homeless people in Orange County. Our goal is to see every homeless person receive three healthy meals each day throughout the entire *40 Days of Community*. We'll need to collect, prepare, and distribute over 1,000 tons of food to accomplish this goal. Every Saddleback small group is encouraged to participate in this enormous project. We'll talk about this in greater detail next week, but we just want to get it on your radar screen in this session. Start discussing the idea right now and answer the question, "Why is it important for your group to reach out to the community with the love of Christ?"

WORSHIP TOGETHER . . . . .10 MINUTES

1. In simple, one-sentence prayers take a few moments to thank God for his love. If praying aloud with people is new or awkward for you, feel free to pray silently.

*2. One of the best ways to show each other love is to pray for each other. Share your prayer requests with your small group and then take time to pray together. Be sure to pray for friends and loved ones who are seeking God. Record your prayer requests on the *Small Group Prayer and Praise Report* on page 233 of this workbook. Keeping track of group prayer requests and answers to prayer would be a great job for someone in your group. Any volunteers?

BEFORE YOU LEAVE

1. Take a few minutes to look at the *Small Group Calendar* in the *Small Group Resources* section, page 236 of this workbook. Healthy groups share responsibilities and group ownership. Fill out the calendar together, noting where you will meet each week, who will facilitate your discussion time, and who will provide a meal or snack. Note special events, such as birthdays, anniversaries, socials, etc. Coordinating these details would be another great job for someone in the group.

2. Collect phone numbers and email addresses from your small group members. The group roster (called *My Small Group*) on page 238 of your workbook is a good place to keep this information. Pass your workbooks around the circle and have your group members fill in their contact information. New on our website is a **HostHome/GroupHome** page where you can record phone numbers, email addresses, and other important information. Go to **www.saddlebackfamily.com** to check out this tool.

SESSION TWO
Reaching out together

2

CONNECT TOGETHER . . . . .10 MINUTES

1. Welcome any people who are new to your group this week.

*2. Check your progress on last week's group assignment to show love and appreciation to a church staff member or volunteer.

3. How are you progressing with your personal commitment from last week to reach out to someone with the love of Jesus Christ? Did you get started? If so, how did it go?

4. Would anyone like to tell the group about an answer to prayer or something they are learning from their *Better Together* daily devotional readings? Be sure to record answers to prayer in the *Small Group Prayer and Praise Report* on page 233 of this workbook.

GROW TOGETHER . . . . .45 MINUTES

Memory Verse

"Be wise in the way you act with people who are not believers, making the most of every opportunity."

Colossians 4:5 (NCV)

Watch the video lesson now and follow along in your outline.

Reaching out together

"Love is kind." 1 Corinthians 13:4 (NIV)

"'Send the people away so they can go to the surrounding countryside and villages and buy themselves something to eat.' [37]But Jesus answered, 'You give them something to eat.' They said to him, 'That would take eight months of a man's wages! Are we to go and spend that much on bread and give it to them to eat?' [38] 'How many loaves do you have?' he asked. 'Go and see.' When they found out, they said, 'Five—and two fish.' [39] Then Jesus directed them to have all the people sit down in groups...of hundreds and fifties. [41] Taking the five loaves and the two fish and looking up to heaven, he gave thanks and broke the loaves. Then he gave them to his disciples to set before the people. He also divided the two fish among them all. [42] They all ate and were satisfied, [43] and the disciples picked up twelve basketfuls of broken pieces of bread and fish. [44] The number of the men who had eaten was five thousand." Mark 6:36-44 (NIV)

Meeting the Needs of Others

- Recognize the _____need_____.

- Take _____inventory_____.

  "My grace is sufficient for you, for my power is made perfect in weakness."
  2 Corinthians 12:9 (NIV)

- Get _____organized_____.

- Measure the _need_.

- Prepare your _heart_.

"God will give you much, so that you can give away much, and when we take your gifts to those who need them they will break out into thanksgiving and praise to God for your help." 2 Corinthians 9:11 (LB)

- Be _available_.

"Do not merely listen to the word, and so deceive yourselves. Do what it says." James 1:22 (NIV)

"Those you help will be glad not only because of your generous gifts to themselves and to others, but they will praise God for this proof that your deeds are as good as your doctrine." 2 Corinthians 9:13 (LB)

DISCUSSION QUESTIONS

HOST TIP: If your group has eight or more members, we suggest you break into subgroups of three or four people for greater participation and deeper discussion. At the end of the discussion time, come back together and have someone from each group report on the highlights of their discussions.

HOST TIP: This week there are just two questions in this section because we want you to spend most of your discussion time working on the Share Together section of the study.

1. James 1:22 tells us it's not enough just to know truth. We have to put it into practice. And 2 Corinthians 9:11 says our deeds should be *"as good as our doctrine."* What does this mean on a practical level? How do these truths relate to sharing your faith?

*2. Pastor Rick said, "God wants to use your small group to reach the world for Jesus Christ. If you want to know God's plan for solving the world's problems look around the room. You're it. You are God's plan...God works through his people—through physical, tangible demonstrations of compassion, mercy and care." What do you think about that statement? Does it excite you, scare you, or overwhelm you? Why?

HOST TIP: There will be no Serve Together questions this week. We want you to focus the rest of your time on the Share Together section of your study.

SHARE TOGETHER .25 MINUTES

 God wants to use your small group to reach out to the world for Jesus Christ. To discover how, follow the six steps from Pastor Rick's message this week:

*1. **Recognize the need.** The mission staff of Saddleback Church has identified a great need in Orange County: 35,000 homeless people. It is estimated that 70% (or 25,000) of the homeless are families with children. They are often forced to choose between buying groceries and other essentials for survival. These families consist mainly of the working poor who live in run down motels. The motels are places with rampant drugs, prostitution, and crime—obviously no place to raise a healthy family.

Homelessness is on the rise in Orange County. Since 1998 the number of homeless has doubled. It is also estimated that nearly 50,000 more people are at risk of becoming homeless due to substance abuse, mental illness, and a lack of housing options.

Saddleback Church is attacking this startling community need. We have committed to collect, sort, and distribute enough food to provide three meals a day to the entire homeless population in our county during *40 Days of Community.*

2. **Take inventory.** What talents, abilities, experiences, and resources exist in your group to help attack this need? Our food drive is comprised of three parts. Your small group may serve in one, two, or all three aspects.

   a. Collecting food donations at area grocery stores for a weekend

   b. Sorting and boxing at the Tustin Marine Base warehouse

   c. Distributing boxed food directly to the homeless

3. **Get organized.** Your small group may register to participate online at **www.saddlebackfamily.com**. Each person can get the specific training needed in one of two ways. First, a separate *40 Days of Community* Outreach Project video and manual have been provided for each person to take home and review. Second, the training is also viewable online at **www.saddlebackfamily.com**.

4. **Measure the need.** Pastor Rick said, "You'll never know what God can do through you until you come to the end of yourself—until you face a hungry crowd with only a sack lunch." Our hungry crowd is 35,000 homeless people. Your small group's "sack lunch" will be multiplied by thousands of other small groups' efforts that God will bless to provide an abundance for the homeless of Orange County.

5&6. **Prepare your heart** and **Be available**. We will talk about these last two points in the Worship Together section.

WORSHIP TOGETHER . . . . .10 MINUTES

1. **Prepare your heart.** The Bible says in 1 Chronicles 29:14 that everything we have was given to us by God. In silent or spoken prayer, thank God for what he has given you and then offer it back to him to do with as he will.

*2. **Be available.** Romans 12:1 tells us to worship God by offering our bodies to him as living sacrifices. In prayer, offer yourselves to God. Ask him to give you strength and courage to step out in faith as you join together in your community outreach project.

3. Pray for each other's prayer requests. Pray especially for the people you are inviting to come to your small group or Saddleback Church with you. Be sure your Prayer Coordinator records the group's prayer requests on the *Small Group Prayer and Praise Report* on page 233 of this workbook.

BEFORE YOU LEAVE

Was anyone missing from your group this week? If someone was absent, ask for a volunteer from the group to call or email that person and let them know they were missed. It's very important for people to know they are cared about.

SESSION THREE

Belonging together

CONNECT TOGETHER . . . . .10 MINUTES

HOST TIP: If your group is unable to work through the entire session, we have recommended one question or activity with an asterisk (*) in each section of the study.

*1. How do you feel about Saddleback's *40 Days of Community* Outreach Project to feed 35,000 homeless in Orange County? Is it overwhelming to you? Are your plans coming together for your group's participation? Are there any loose ends that need to be tied down?

2. Who has blessed you by meeting a practical need in your life? How did their kindness make you feel?

GROW TOGETHER .45 MINUTES

Memory Verse
"Since we are all one body in Christ, we belong to each other, and each of us needs all the others."

Romans 12:5b (NLT)

Watch the video lesson now and follow along in your outline

Belonging together

"Two are better than one, because they have a good return for their work: If one falls down, his friend can help him up. But pity the man who falls and has no one to help him up...Though one may be overpowered, two can defend themselves. A cord of three strands is not quickly broken." Ecclesiastes 4:9-12 (NIV)

Lessons on Love from 1 Corinthians 13:7

- Love always _____.

  "A gossip betrays a confidence but a trustworthy man keeps a secret." Proverbs 11:13 (NIV)

  Protects = _____

- Love always _____.

  We believe _____ each other...we believe _____ each other.

- Love always _____.

  Be _____ about other people's accomplishments.

- Love always _____.

  "Some friendships do not last, but some friends are more loyal than brothers." Proverbs 18:24 (GNB)

  "In Christ, we who are many form one body, and each member belongs to all the others." Romans 12:5 (NIV)

DISCUSSION QUESTIONS

HOST TIP: If your group has eight or more members, we suggest you break into subgroups of three or four people for greater participation and deeper discussion.

For this week's study, please subgroup into separate groups of men and women.

*1. Which of the four statements about love from 1 Corinthians 13:7 spoke to you most powerfully? Why? How can you apply these truths to your personal life this week?

2. What can we do to apply these truths to our group life? What does it mean to really trust each other and to persevere in our relationships together? What can we do to build trust and foster hope within our group?

3. Talk about a time when you needed the faith of your friends to lift you in prayer, or a time when God answered your prayers for someone else.

4. Have one or two group members share their story of how they came to Christ and the role friendship played in their decision.

SERVE TOGETHER . . . . 10 MINUTES

*1. A recent survey revealed that the number one characteristic of a growing church is the atmosphere of love among the membership. How would you describe the atmosphere of love in your church (welcoming, warm, safe, impersonal, cliquey, etc.)? What can your small group do to help build a more loving community in your church?

2. Have you taken CLASS 101 at Saddleback Church and signed the membership covenant? If some members of your group have not had the chance yet, consider attending the next scheduled CLASS 101 as a group to support one another. The next CLASS 101 is Sunday, November 14 from 3–7:30 PM. Childcare is available and dinner is provided.

SHARE TOGETHER . . . . 15 MINUTES

1. Your group outreach project can be a great conversation starter for inviting seekers as well as Christ-following friends to join your small group. When people express interest or curiosity about your project, invite them to join you at your next group meeting to find out more about it. Who can you tell about your group outreach project this week?

*2. Think of a friend who is not currently connected to a church. Why not invite that person to come to Saddleback Church with you this weekend? What is the worst thing that could happen if you invite them? What is the best thing that could happen if you invite them? Is the potential benefit worth the risk? Remember, over 90% of Christians first went to church because a friend or family member invited them. Tell your group the name of at least one person who you will invite to church or to your next small group meeting.

_____

Name

_____

Name

WORSHIP TOGETHER ....10 MINUTES

1. Would anyone like to share an answer to a prayer from last week? Be sure to record answers to prayer in the *Small Group Prayer and Praise Report* on page 233 of this workbook.

2. Pray for your small group outreach project.

*3. Love requires us to believe *in* each other and *for* each other. Pair up with a spiritual partner for the rest of your prayer time. A spiritual partner is someone we can talk to about our spiritual growth and "call for back-up" when we need prayer support. Take a moment to select someone in your group to be your spiritual partner for the remaining weeks of this study. (We strongly recommend that men partner with men and women partner with women.) After you have paired up, pray for each other's requests. Plan to check in with each other by phone, email, or over coffee at least once before your next small group meeting. This could be a great time to pray for each other during the coming week, and share what you are learning from your *Better Together* daily devotional reading.

SESSION FOUR
Growing together

days of
community

CONNECT TOGETHER ....10 MINUTES

HOST TIP: If your group is unable to work through the entire session, we have recommended one question or activity with an asterisk (*) in each section of the study.

1. Have you had a chance to invite a friend or family member to Saddleback Church or to your small group yet? How did they respond?

*2. Would anyone like to share something you learned this week from your *Better Together* devotional reading?

3. Who have been some of the greatest examples of Christian love for you?

GROW TOGETHER ....50 MINUTES

Memory Verse
"Encourage one another and build each other up."
1 Thessalonians 5:11 (NIV)

Watch the video lesson now and follow along in your outline.

Growing together

1. Growing together requires _____.

   "Love is patient…It is not rude…it is not easily angered." 1 Corinthians 13:4-5 (NIV)

   "Be humble and gentle in every way. Be patient with each other and lovingly accept each other." Ephesians 4:2 (GW)

2. Growing together requires _____.

   "Love rejoices in the truth." 1 Corinthians 13:6a (CEV)

   "Speak the truth in a spirit of love." Ephesians 4:15 (TEV)

Speaking the Truth in Love

- Check your _____.

   "Why worry about a speck in your friend's eye when you have a log in your own?…First get rid of the log in your own eye; then perhaps you will see well enough to deal with the speck in your friend's eye." Matthew 7:3-5 (NLT)

- Plan your _____.

   Plan _____ you'll say it.

   "The right word at the right time is like precious gold set in silver." Proverbs 25:11 (CEV)

   Plan _____ you'll say.

   "A wise friend's kind reprimand is like a gold ring slipped on your finger." Proverbs 25:12 (Msg.)

Plan _____ you'll say it.

"Thoughtless words can wound as deeply as any sword, but wisely spoken words can heal." Proverbs 12:18 (TEV)

- _____.

- Say it _____.

"A wise mature person is known for his understanding. The more pleasant his words, the more persuasive he is." Proverbs 16:21 (TEV)

- Say it _____.

- Say it _____.

"A soft answer turns away wrath." Proverbs 15:1a (NKJV)

"If someone is trapped in sin, you should gently lead that person back to the right path." Galatians 6:1 (CEV)

"An honest answer is a sign of a true friendship." Proverbs 24:26 (TEV)

3. Growing together requires _____.

"Love keeps no record of wrongs." 1 Corinthians 13:5b (NIV)

"Bear with each other and forgive whatever grievances you may have against one another. Forgive as the Lord forgave you." Colossians 3:13 (NIV)

"In the same way you judge others, you will be judged, and with the measure you use, it will be measured to you." Matthew 7:2 (NIV)

DISCUSSION QUESTIONS

HOST TIP: If your group has eight or more members, we suggest you break into subgroups of three or four people for greater participation and deeper discussion. At the end of the discussion time, come back together and have someone from each group report on the highlights of their discussions.

*1. This lesson covered three aspects of love that can sometimes be very difficult: patience, truthfulness, and forgiveness. Which part of the lesson was most meaningful to you? Why?

2. Where does impatience show up in your life?

3. What is the difference between judging people and confronting them in love?

4. How do you respond when someone hurts you? Why is it so hard to forgive people who hurt us? What are the consequences of choosing not to forgive?

SERVE TOGETHER . . . . .10 MINUTES

1. In what ways do patience, truthfulness and forgiveness impact your ability to serve in ministry?

*2. Is there someone in your church or small group with whom you need to seek reconciliation? Why wait any longer? Reach out to that person this week with truthfulness and forgiveness. We will pray together about these relationships during the Worship Together section of this study.

SHARE TOGETHER . . . . .10 MINUTES

*1. How can unforgiveness or resentment in your relationship with someone who is not a follower of Christ affect their openness to Jesus Christ? What difference could a healed relationship make in that person's life?

2. How do unity and love in your church affect your church's testimony to your community?

WORSHIP TOGETHER . . . . .10 MINUTES

1. As Pastor Rick closed his message, he asked: "Do you need to be patient with someone? Do you need to speak the truth in love to someone? Do you need to forgive someone?" Take a moment to quietly reflect on these questions. Write down a name or a situation that comes to mind.

_____

Name or Situation

*2. Break into subgroups of three or four people, or pair up with your spiritual partner. Tell each other if you have a relationship that needs healing, either through patience, truthfulness or forgiveness. This is not a time to share details or assign blame. Simply mention the person's name or the nature of the relationship (e.g., brother, colleague, mother, neighbor, friend, etc). Share as openly as you feel comfortable so the group can pray more specifically for you. Then, as an act of worship and because it will please the Father, pray for each other, asking God to soften your hearts and give you courage and grace to initiate the healing process. If you are not yet ready to reconcile, then pray that God will help you to become "willing to be ready."

BEFORE YOU LEAVE

Recruit a volunteer to be your Group Ministry Project Coordinator! His or her job will be to check out *Rick's Picks* online at **www.saddlebackfamily.com** to discover great ministry opportunities for your small group to serve our church family together. You will need this information for next week's small group meeting,

SESSION FIVE
Serving together

CONNECT TOGETHER . . . . .10 MINUTES

HOST TIP: If your group is unable to work through the entire session, we have recommended one question or activity with an asterisk (*) in each section of the study.

*1. Check the progress of your group outreach project.

2. Last week we talked and prayed about being patient with others, speaking the truth in love, and forgiveness. How did that lesson impact your life this week? Did you see any answers to your prayer?

3. This week we are going to talk about serving the Lord by serving people in your church family at Saddleback. What do you think are the characteristics of a true servant?

GROW TOGETHER . . . . .45 MINUTES

Memory Verse
*"By helping each other with your troubles,
you truly obey the law of Christ."*

Galatians 6:2 (NCV)

Watch the video lesson now and follow along in your outline.

Serving together

Four Key Aspects of Serving Together

Groups that serve together:

1. Make themselves _____ to serve.

2. Work as a *body*.

   "From him the whole body, joined and held together by every supporting ligament, grows and builds itself up in love, as each part does its work." Ephesians 4:16 (NIV)

3. Think more about *others* than themselves.

   "Forget yourselves long enough to lend a helping hand." Philippians 2:4 (Msg.)

   "...consider how we may spur one another on toward love and good deeds." Hebrews 10:24 (NIV)

4. Do every task with equal _____.

   "If anyone wants to be first, he must be the very last, and the servant of all." Mark 9:35 (NIV)

   "He will not forget how hard you have worked for him and how you have shown your love to him by caring for other Christians." Hebrews 6:10 (NLT)

DISCUSSION QUESTIONS

1. Are you currently serving in a ministry at Saddleback Church? If you are, tell the group about it.

2. Where do you find the most joy when it comes to helping others?

3. The true test of a servant-heart is in how you react when you are treated like a servant. Have you ever been treated like a servant? How did it make you feel?

*4. Consider these roadblocks to ministry: time constraints, overcommitment, lack of interest, lack of confidence, lack of information. Which of these roadblocks presents the biggest obstacle for you? What can you do to avoid or overcome these barriers to ministry?

HOST TIP: There will be no Share Together questions this week. We want you to focus the rest of your time on the Serve Together section of your study.

SERVE TOGETHER .25 MINUTES

What can you do together as a small group to serve your Saddleback Church family?

*1. **Determine a need:** What will your group do? Pastor Rick said, "There is nothing too small, too mundane, or too menial for a true servant." Make a list of practical needs your group can meet here at Saddleback Church. Here are a few examples to get you started:

- Provide meals for a family in need.

- Pray with a church member who is in the hospital.

- Assist senior adults in your church with projects around the house.

- Offer help to military families whose moms or dads are serving overseas.

- Take on a maintenance project at church such as painting or re-carpeting an office or classroom.

- Other:_____

- Other:_____

- Other:_____

Now pray together and ask the Lord what he would have you do. If your group is unable to determine a ministry need together, then check out *Rick's Picks* online at **www.saddlebackfamily.com** to discover great ministry opportunities for your group to serve our church family together.

2. **Develop a plan:** How will you meet the need? When your group has chosen your ministry project, determine your plan of action, identify the tasks, and divide up the responsibilities. If you did not choose a Group Ministry Project Coordinator last week, then select someone this week to fill this crucial role. The Group Ministry Project Coordinator will help move your plan from the talking stage to the action stage.

Task to be done	Who will do it

3. **Decide on a date:** When will you take action? Get out your calendars and choose a date when your group can serve together. Make it sooner than later.

WORSHIP TOGETHER . . . . .10 MINUTES

 *1. Pray for your group ministry project. Commit your plans to the Lord and ask him to direct your steps. Thank God in advance for what he is going to do through you as your group blesses someone in need.

2. Pray this prayer aloud together:

Father, we want to live our lives to please you.

We want to walk through each day depending on your power,

looking for your hand,

and listening for the still, small voice of your guidance.

Use us for your kingdom's purposes.

Nudge us into greater acts of faith.

Call us to a deeper level of trust.

Soften our hearts, O Lord,

so that we may live worthy of your calling

and fulfill your highest purposes for our lives.

We pray these things in the name of Jesus,

and for the glory of your kingdom.

Amen.*

3. Break into subgroups and pray for one another's prayer requests.

*Adapted from The NIV Worship Bible, page 1596. ©2000 The Corinthian Group. All rights reserved. Used by permission.

4. *Optional:* Close your worship time by singing the song, "Trust God."

HOST TIP: The song "Trust God" may be downloaded at no charge at www.EncouragingMusic.com

A word about singing: Some people love to sing together. Some people would rather get a root canal. In this Worship Together section, we have recommended an optional, familiar song for you to sing in your group. Please don't feel obligated to use it. It is only a suggestion for groups that are comfortable singing together. If you have a guitar or keyboard player in your small group and someone who loves to lead singing, then by all means incorporate this song or others into your worship time. If singing together is awkward for your group, simply read the lyrics out loud as a prayer.

Trust God

Trust God
From the bottom of your heart
Don't try to figure out everything on your own
Trust God
For where your life is going
God is in control
God is in control

Commit to the Lord
Whatever you do
And your plans will succeed
Pray, Lord, I'm available to you
Here I am, Lord, use me

Words and Music by Rick Muchow
©2001 Encouraging Music

BEFORE YOU LEAVE

1. Start making plans for an evening meal or a party with your group to celebrate what God has done in your lives through these *40 Days of Community.* A party is an excellent opportunity for you to invite people who might be interested in joining your group. Talk about your celebration before you leave your meeting. Where will you have your party? When will you have it? Will it be a potluck, will someone barbeque, or will you call out for pizza? Divide up the responsibilities and then get ready to enjoy a great time of fellowship together. You deserve it!

2. There is just one week left in *40 Days of Community.* Take a few minutes for an informal evaluation of your small group experience. What has been helpful to you? What has challenged you? What would make this a better experience? How do you feel about continuing on as a group? Talk about these issues and address any concerns that might be raised.

3. If you plan to stay together as a group, which we highly encourage you to do, spend some time talking about what your group will study next. We invite you to visit the Small Group Curriculum table on the patio or come by the Ministry Center to check out the other video-based small group studies that are available from the *Saddleback Bible Study Series.* Next week we will give some specific suggestions.

SESSION SIX
Worshiping together

CONNECT TOGETHER . . . . .10 MINUTES

HOST TIP: If your group is unable to work through the entire session, we have recommended one question or activity with an asterisk (*) in each section of the study.

*1. Check in about the progress of your group's ministry plans that you discussed last week.

2. Would anyone like to tell about an answer to prayer or something they are learning from the *Better Together* daily devotional readings?

3. How would your friends rate you on the generosity meter?

Scrooge---Mother Teresa

Generosity Meter

GROW TOGETHER . . . . .45 MINUTES

Memory Verse
*"You have six days to do your work, but the seventh day
of each week is holy because it belongs to me."*

Leviticus 23:3 (CEV)

**Watch the video lesson now and follow
along in your outline.**

Worshiping together

Six Practical Reasons for Giving

1. Giving makes me more like _____.

   "God so loved the world that he gave..." John 3:16a (NIV)

2. Giving draws me _____ to God.

   "Where your treasure is, there your heart will be also." Matthew 6:21 (NIV)

3. Giving is the antidote to _____.

   "Command those who are rich in this present world not to be arrogant nor to put their hope in wealth, which is so uncertain, but to put their hope in God, who richly provides us with everything for our enjoyment. Command them...to be generous and willing to share. In this way...they may take hold of the life that is truly life." 1 Timothy 6:17-19 (NIV)

4. Giving strengthens my _____.

   "'Bring the whole tithe to the storehouse... Test me in this,' says the Lord Almighty, 'and see if I will not throw open the floodgates of heaven and pour out so much blessing that you will not have room enough for it!'" Malachi 3:10 (NIV)

5. Giving is an investment for _____.

   "Give happily to those in need, always being ready to share...whatever God has given you. By doing this, you will be storing up real treasure for yourself in heaven—it is the only safe investment for eternity." 1 Timothy 6:18-19 (LB)

6. Giving blesses me in _____.

"A generous man will prosper; he who refreshes others will himself be refreshed."
Proverbs 11:25 (NIV)

"There is more happiness in giving than in receiving." Acts 20:35b (NJB)

Four Attitudes for Giving

1. Give _____.

"For if the willingness is there, the gift is acceptable according to what one has, not according to what he does not have." 2 Corinthians 8:12 (NIV)

"Each man should give what he has decided in his heart to give, not reluctantly or under compulsion." 2 Corinthians 9:7 (NIV)

2. Give _____.

"How can I repay the Lord for all his goodness to me?" Psalm 116:12 (NIV)

"Everything comes from you, and we have given you only what comes from your hand." 1 Chronicles 29:14b (NIV)

3. Give _____.

"God loves a cheerful giver." 2 Corinthians 9:7b (NIV)

4. Give _____.

> *"Remember this: whoever sows sparingly will also reap sparingly, and whoever sows generously will also reap generously."* 2 Corinthians 9:6 (NIV)

> *"Just as you excel in everything—in faith, in speech, in knowledge, in complete earnestness and in your love for us—see that you also excel in this grace of giving."* 2 Corinthians 8:7 (NIV)

DISCUSSION QUESTIONS

*1. Take a few minutes to share what your relationships in this group have meant to you.

2. What are some practical ways you can demonstrate your gratitude to God?

3. Jesus said it is better to give than receive. Share about a time you found this to be true in your own life. How did giving make you feel?

4. Why do you think generosity is so important to God?

SERVE TOGETHER . . . . .10 MINUTES

*1. In this session we've talked about giving financially. But another way for us to give is through the use of our time. What can you do to continue serving your church together as a group?

2. One person in your group who has seen a need and seized the opportunity to meet it is your small group host. His or her leadership in your group has provided an example of using one's gifts to serve others. Take a few minutes to affirm your host. Focus on the character qualities, gifts, and talents he or she brings to your group. Thank your host for all of his or her hard work.

SHARE TOGETHER . . . . .10 MINUTES

*1. We want to encourage you to continue to develop the purpose of evangelism in your small group life. We pray your project will be the starting point of a lifestyle of service for your group and for you as an individual. Our hope is that you will look back after these 40 days and not say, "Look what we did," but rather say, "Look what we started!" What can your group do to continue reaching out to your community with the love of Jesus Christ?

2. Pastor Rick would love to hear about your small group's ministry and outreach projects. Please email your stories to **stories@purposedriven.com**. Thanks!

WORSHIP TOGETHER . . . . .15 MINUTES

*1. What has been the most important lesson you have learned through *40 Days of Community*? Have each member of the group share something that has been meaningful to him or her. Then offer prayers of thanks together for what God has done in your lives.

2. Close your time together by praying for each other's prayer requests. Recognize and celebrate any answered prayers from previous weeks. Record your prayer requests on the *Small Group Prayer and Praise Report* on page 233 of this workbook.

BEFORE YOU LEAVE

1. If you haven't already done so, take some time now to talk about your future together as a small group. We hope you will continue meeting together, now that you know what it is like to live in community. Where will you go from here? When and where will you meet? What will you study? Is there anything you want to do differently in your group life? If your host agreed to lead your group temporarily for these forty days and is planning to return to his or her previous small group, who will be your new host? Address these questions before you finish up today.

For your next small group study, we suggest you pick up *A Fresh Look at Jesus*, a two-week study about the life of Jesus Christ. This is a great study for your group as you get ready for the Christmas season.

In January there will be several new studies from the *Saddleback Bible Study Series* including:
> • *Sermon on the Mount, Volume 1.* Pastor Lance Witt takes a close look at the most famous of Jesus' sermons. This is the first volume of a four volume series.

> • *Serving God Together:* This eight week series reveals key practices for small groups if they are to move out and serve together. A great follow-up to *40 Days of Community*, and a must for small groups considering a PEACE Plan trip.

These, and other studies, are available on the patio at the Small Group Curriculum table or during the week in the Ministry Center for pick up by small group hosts.

2. We encourage you to have a party or celebration together—a time to focus on fellowship and celebrate what God has done throughout the last several weeks. This gathering is also a good opportunity to bring friends who might want to join your small group. It gives potential group members a nonthreatening environment in which to get acquainted with the rest of you. Talk about this with your group: Set a date, time, and location, and decide what kind of food you will have.

GROUP
DEVELOPMENT

Small Group Resources

TOP TEN HELPS FOR HOSTS
Ideas for helping your group succeed

Congratulations. As the Host of your small group, you have responded to the call to help shepherd Jesus' flock. Few other tasks in the family of God surpass the contribution you will be making.

On the curriculum videotape or DVD, you will find *Helps for Hosts* that offer insights and coaching for facilitating each week's session. Each *Helps for Hosts* feature is taught by Pastor Rick Warren and is 3-5 minutes long.

As you prepare to facilitate your group, whether it is one session or the entire series, here are a few additional thoughts to keep in mind. We encourage you to read and review these tips with each new discussion host before he or she leads.

1. **Remember you are not alone.** God knows everything about you, and he knew you would be asked to facilitate your group. Even though you may not feel ready, this is common for all good hosts. God promises, *"I will never leave you; I will never abandon you"* (Hebrews 13:5, TEV). Whether you are facilitating for one evening, several weeks, or a lifetime, you will be blessed as you serve.

2. **Don't try to do it alone.** Pray right now for God to help you build a healthy team. If you can enlist a co-host to help you shepherd the group, you will find your experience much richer. This is your chance to involve as many people as you can in building a healthy group. All you have to do is ask people to help. You'll be surprised at the response.

3. **Be friendly and be yourself.** God wants to use your unique gifts and temperament. Be sure to greet people at the door with a big smile…this can set the mood for the whole gathering. Remember, they are taking as big a step as you are to show up at your house! Don't try to do things exactly like another host; do them in a way that fits you. Admit when you don't have an answer and apologize when you make a mistake. Your group will love you for it and you'll sleep better at night.

TOP TEN HELPS FOR HOSTS
Ideas for helping your group succeed (continued)

4. **Prepare for your meeting ahead of time.** Review the session and the video *Helps for Hosts*. Write down your responses to each question. Pay special attention to exercises that ask group members to do something other than engage in discussion. These exercises will help your group live what the Bible teaches, not just talk about it. If the exercise employs one of the items in the *Small Group Resources* section (such as the *Group Guidelines*), be sure to look over that item so you'll know how it works.

5. **Pray for your group members by name.** Before you begin your session, take a few moments and pray for each member by name. You may want to review the prayer list at least once a week. Ask God to use your time together to touch the heart of every person in your group. Expect God to lead you to whomever he wants you to encourage or challenge in a special way. If you listen, God will surely lead.

6. **When you ask a question, be patient.** Someone will eventually respond. Sometimes people need a moment or two of silence to think about the question. If silence doesn't bother you, it won't bother anyone else. After someone responds, affirm the response with a simple "thanks" or "great answer." Then ask, "How about somebody else?" or "Would someone who hasn't shared like to add anything?" Be sensitive to new people or reluctant members who aren't ready to say, pray, or do anything. If you give them a safe setting, they will blossom over time. If someone in your group is a "wall flower" who sits silently through every session, consider talking to them privately and encouraging them to participate. Let them know how important they are to you—that they are loved and appreciated, and that the group would value their input. Remember, still water often runs deep.

7. **Provide transitions between questions.** Ask if anyone would like to read the paragraph or Bible passage. Don't call on anyone, but ask for a volunteer, and then be patient until someone begins. Be sure to thank the person who reads aloud.

8. **Break into smaller groups occasionally.** The Grow Together and Worship Together sections provide good opportunities to break into smaller circles of 3-5 people. With a greater opportunity to talk in a small circle, people will connect more with the study, apply more quickly what they're learning, and ultimately get more out of their small group experience. A small circle also encourages a quiet person to participate and tends to minimize the effects of a more vocal or dominant member.

   Small circles are also helpful during prayer time. People who are unaccustomed to praying aloud will feel more comfortable trying it with just two or three others. Also, prayer requests won't take as much time, so circles will have more time to actually pray. When you gather back with the whole group, you can have one person from each circle briefly update everyone on the prayer requests from their sub-groups. The other great aspect of sub-grouping is that it fosters leadership development. As you ask people in the group to facilitate discussion or to lead a prayer circle, it gives them a small leadership step that can build their confidence.

9. **Rotate facilitators occasionally.** You may be perfectly capable of hosting each time, but you will help others grow in their faith and gifts if you give them opportunities to host the group.

10. **One final challenge** (for new or first-time hosts): Before your first opportunity to lead, read each of the six passages listed below as a devotional exercise to help prepare you with a shepherd's heart. Trust us on this one. If you do this, you will be more than ready for your first meeting.

   • Matthew 9:36-38
   "When Jesus saw the crowds, he had compassion on them, because they were harassed and helpless, like sheep without a shepherd. Then he said to his disciples, 'The harvest is plentiful but the workers are few. Ask the Lord of the harvest, therefore, to send out workers into his harvest field.'"

- John 10:14-15

  "I am the good shepherd; I know my sheep and my sheep know me—just as the Father knows me and I know the Father—and I lay down my life for the sheep."

- 1 Peter 5:2-4

  "Be shepherds of God's flock that is under your care, serving as overseers—not because you must, but because you are willing, as God wants you to be; not greedy for money, but eager to serve; not lording it over those entrusted to you, but being examples to the flock. And when the Chief Shepherd appears, you will receive the crown of glory that will never fade away."

- Philippians 2:1-5

  "If you have any encouragement from being united with Christ, if any comfort from his love, if any fellowship with the Spirit, if any tenderness and compassion, then make my joy complete by being like-minded, having the same love, being one in spirit and purpose. Do nothing out of selfish ambition or vain conceit, but in humility consider others better than yourselves. Each of you should look not only to your own interests, but also to the interests of others. Your attitude should be the same as that of Jesus Christ."

- Hebrews 10:23-25

  "Let us hold unswervingly to the hope we profess, for he who promised is faithful. And let us consider how we may spur one another on toward love and good deeds. Let us not give up meeting together, as some are in the habit of doing, but let us encourage one another—and all the more as you see the Day approaching."

- 1 Thessalonians 2:7,8, 11-12

  "But we were gentle among you, like a mother caring for her little children. We loved you so much that we were delighted to share with you not only the Gospel of God but our lives as well, because you had become so dear to us...For you know that we dealt with each of you as a father deals with his own children, encouraging, comforting and urging you to live lives worthy of God, who calls you into his kingdom and glory."

FREQUENTLY ASKED QUESTIONS

How long will this group meet?
Your *40 Days of Community* small group will meet for six weeks. We encourage your group to add a seventh session for a celebration. In your final session, each group member may decide if he or she desires to continue on for another study. At that time you may also want to do some informal evaluation, discuss your Group Guidelines, and decide which study you want to do next. We recommend you visit our website at **www.saddlebackfamily.com** for more video-based small group studies.

Who is the host?
The host is the person who coordinates and facilitates your group meetings. In addition to a host, we encourage you to select one or more group members to lead your group discussions. Several other responsibilities can be rotated, including refreshments, prayer requests, worship, or keeping up with those who miss a meeting. Shared ownership in the group helps everybody grow.

Where do we find new group members?
Recruiting new members can be a challenge for groups, especially new groups with just a few people, or existing groups that lose a few people along the way. We encourage you to use the *Circles of Life* diagram on page 232 of this workbook to brainstorm a list of people from your workplace, church, school, neighborhood, family, and so on. Then pray for the people on each member's list. Allow each member to invite several people from their list. Some groups fear that newcomers will interrupt the intimacy that members have built over time. However, groups that welcome newcomers generally gain strength with the infusion of new blood. Remember, the next person you add just might become a friend for eternity. Logistically, groups find different ways to add members. Some groups remain permanently open, while others choose to open periodically, such as at the beginning or end of a study. If your group becomes too large for easy, face-to-face conversations, you can sub-group, forming a second discussion group in another room.

How do we handle the childcare needs in our group?
Childcare needs must be handled very carefully. This is a sensitive issue. We suggest you seek creative solutions as a group. One common solution is to have the adults meet in the living room and share the cost of a babysitter (or two) who can be with the kids in another part of the house. Another popular option is to have one home for the kids and a second home (close by) for the adults. If desired, the adults could rotate the responsibility of providing a lesson for the kids. This last option is great with school age kids and can be a huge blessing to families.

SADDLEBACK CHURCH GROUP GUIDELINES

It's a good idea for every group to put words to their shared values, expectations, and commitments. Such guidelines will help you avoid unspoken agendas and unmet expectations. We recommend you discuss your guidelines during Session One in order to lay the foundation for a healthy group experience. Feel free to add anything that is important to your group. If the idea of a written agreement is unfamiliar to your group, we encourage you to give it a try.

WE AGREE TO THE FOLLOWING VALUES:

Clear Purpose To grow healthy, spiritual lives by building a healthy small group community

Group Attendance To give priority to the group meeting (call if I am absent or late)

Safe Environment To create a safe place where people can be heard and feel loved (no quick answers, snap judgments, or simple fixes)

Be Confidential To keep anything that is shared strictly confidential and within the group

Conflict Resolution To avoid gossip and to immediately resolve any concerns by following the principles of Matt. 18:15-17 which begins with going directly to the person with whom you have an issue

Spiritual Health To give group members permission to help me live a healthy, balanced spiritual life that is pleasing to God

Limit Our Freedom To limit our freedom by not serving or consuming alcohol during Saddleback small group meetings or events so as to avoid causing a weaker brother or sister to stumble (1 Cor 8:1-13, Rom 14:19-21)

Welcome Newcomers To invite our friends who might benefit from this study and warmly welcome newcomers

Building Relationships To get to know the other members of the group and pray for them regularly

Other _____

We agree on the following items:

• Refreshments/Mealtimes _____

• Childcare _____

• When we will meet (day of week) _____

• Where we will meet (place) _____

• We will begin at (time) _____ and end at _____

• We will do our best (some or all) to attend the following service together: ❏ Sat 4:30 pm ❏ Sat 6:30 pm ❏ Sun 9:00 am ❏ Sun 11:15 am ❏ Sun 4:30 pm ❏ Sun 6:30 pm

• Review date of this agreement _____

CIRCLES OF LIFE
Small Group Connections

DISCOVER WHO YOU CAN CONNECT IN COMMUNITY

Use this chart to help carry out one of the values in the Group Guidelines, to "Welcome Newcomers."

"Follow me and I will make you fishers of men." Matthew 4:19

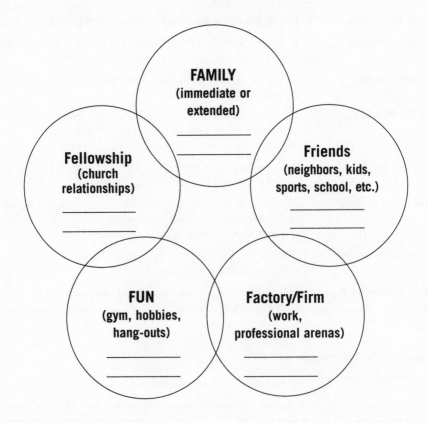

Follow this simple three-step process:

1. List 1-2 people in each circle.

2. Prayerfully select one person or couple from your list and tell your group about them.

3. Give them a call and invite them to your next meeting. Over fifty percent of those invited to a small group say, "Yes!"

SMALL GROUP
Prayer and Praise Report

This is a place where you can write each other's requests for prayer. You can also make a note when God answers a prayer. Pray for each other's requests. If you're new to group prayer, it's okay to pray silently or to pray by using just one sentence: "God, please help _____ to _____."

DATE	PERSON	PRAYER REQUEST	PRAISE REPORT

SMALL GROUP
Prayer and Praise Report

DATE	PERSON	PRAYER REQUEST	PRAISE REPORT

SMALL GROUP
Prayer and Praise Report

DATE	PERSON	PRAYER REQUEST	PRAISE REPORT

SMALL GROUP CALENDAR

Healthy groups share responsibilities and group ownership. It might take some time for this to develop. Shared ownership ensures that responsibility for the group doesn't fall to one person. Use the calendar to keep track of social events, mission projects, birthdays, or days off. Complete this calendar at your first or second meeting. Planning ahead will increase attendance and shared ownership.

DATE	LESSON	LOCATION	FACILITATOR	SNACK OR MEAL
10/22	Session 2	Steve & Laura's	Bill Jones	John & Alice

ANSWER KEY
For sessions one through six

SESSION ONE
What matters most

Nothing I say will matter.

Nothing I know will matter.

Nothing I believe will matter.

Nothing I give will matter.

Nothing I accomplish will matter.

Love is a command.

Love is a choice.

Love is a conduct.

Love is a commitment.

SESSION TWO
Reaching out together

Recognize the need.

Take inventory.

Get organized.

Measure the need.

Prepare your heart.

Be available.

SESSION THREE
Belonging together

Love always protects.

Protects = cover over with silence

Love always trusts.

We believe in each other...
  we believe for each other.

Love always hopes.

Be enthusiastic about other
  people's accomplishments.

Love always perseveres.

SESSION FOUR
Growing together

Growing together requires patience.

Growing together requires truthfulness.

Check your motives.

Plan your presentation.

Plan when you'll say it.

Plan what you'll say.

Plan how you'll say it.

Pray.

Say it tactfully.

Say it lovingly.

Say it gently.

Growing together requires forgiveness.

SESSION FIVE
Serving together

Make themselves available to serve.

Work as a team.

Think more about others than themselves.

Do every task with equal dedication.

SESSION SIX
Worshiping together

Giving makes me more like God.

Giving draws me closer to God.

Giving is the antidote to materialism.

Giving strengthens my faith.

Giving is an investment for eternity.

Giving blesses me in return.

Give willingly.

Give thankfully.

Give joyfully.

Give expectantly.

MY SMALL GROUP
Roster and contact information

	NAME	HOME PHONE	EMAIL
1.			
2.			
3.			
4.			
5.			
6.			
7.			
8.			
9.			
10.			
11.			
12.			
13.			